THE DON'T SWEAT GUIDE
FOR WEDDINGS

Other books by the editors of Don't Sweat Press

The Don't Sweat Affirmations
The Don't Sweat Guide for Couples
The Don't Sweat Guide for Graduates
The Don't Sweat Guide for Grandparents
The Don't Sweat Guide for Parents
The Don't Sweat Guide for Moms

THE DON'T SWEAT GUIDE
FOR WEDDINGS

Get More Enjoyment Out of One of the Most Important Events in Your Life

By the Editors of Don't Sweat Press
Foreword by Richard Carlson, Ph.D.,
author of the bestselling *Don't Sweat the Small Stuff*

New York

Hyperion books are available for special promotions and premiums.
For details contact Hyperion Special Markets, 77 West 66th Street,
11th floor, New York, New York, 10023, or call 212-456-0100.

Copyright © 2002 Carlson, LLC.

All rights reserved. No part of this book may be used or reproduced
in any manner whatsoever without the written permission of the Publisher.
Printed in the United States of America. For information address:
Hyperion, 77 W. 66th Street, New York, New York 10023-6298.

ISBN 0-7868-8726-5

FIRST EDITION

10 9 8 7 6 5 4 3 2 1

Contents

Foreword   11

1. Make a Date with Your Fiancé   15

2. Get a Grip—Start with the Basics   17

3. Come to Terms with Religious Differences   19

4. Give Yourself the Gift of Backup Planning   21

5. Play the Numbers Game   23

6. Share the News   25

7. Take Pride in Your Engagement Ring   27

8. Your Wedding Is Your Priority   29

9. Explore Theme Weddings   30

10. Have the Courage to Break Tradition   31

11. Embrace New Tradition   33

12. Show Your Personality   35

13. Consider Hiring a Professional   36

14. Do You Prefer a Child-Free Wedding?   38

15. Your Wedding Organizer   40

16. Treat Your Wedding Like a Business   42

17. Appreciate Your Beloved for Who He Is   44

18. Learn to Say Yes   46

19. Get Help for the Honeymoon   48

20. Celebrate Your Choice of Bridesmaids   50

21. Honor Those Whom You Cherish   52

22. Make Peace with Your Guest List   54

23. Handle Coworkers and Acquaintances with Grace   56

24. Forgo the Wedding Announcements   58

25. Find the Perfect Dress   60

26. Don't Stress over Writing Your Vows   62

27. The Wedding Rings   64

28. Come to Terms with the Prenuptials   66

29. The Name Change   68

30. Engage Yourself in a Party   70

31. Know Your Budget   72

32. Specify Your Funding   74

33. Be Flexible with Funds   76

34. List Your Priorities   78

35. Restructure Your Plans   80

36. Seek Creative Solutions   82

37. Keep Simplicity in Mind   83

38. Be Sensitive to the Feelings of Your Parents   85

39. More Specific Now, Less Stressed Later   87

40. Learn to Say No   89

41. Plan and Protect Your Beauty Confidence   91

42. Indulge Yourself in the Menu   93

43. Set the Mood with Music   95

44. Preserve Your Wedding Memories   97

45. Break Away from Bridal Guilt   99

46. Rule the Weight Game   101

47. Honor Your Body   103

48. Don't Listen to the "What Ifs"   105

49. He May Not Be Detail-Oriented   107

50. Recognize the Most Valuable Wedding Gifts   109

51. Release Doubt   111

52. Speak Up When It Becomes Too Much   113

53. Express Your Feelings   115

54. Let Go of the Details   117

55. Distinguish Good Advice from Bad Advice   119

56. Let Go of Other People's Conflicts   121

57. Ask for What You Want   123

58. Remember Personal Priorities in Your Budget   125

59. Succeed at Long-Distance Planning   127

60. Embrace Visiting Guests from a Distance   130

61. Give from Your Heart to the Wedding Party   132

62. Consider Skipping the Attendants' Parties   134

63. Include Your Children in the Celebration   136

64. Negotiate with the Underwriter   138

65. Create a Paperwork Date Night   140

66. Let Your Friends Shower You with Attention   142

67. Acknowledge the Bachelor Party with Grace   144

68. Enjoy a Bachelorette Party   146

69. Pack for Freedom on Your Honeymoon   148

70. Share Your Joy   150

71. Don't Trade Away Your Future   152

72. You Can't Make Everybody Happy   154

73. Have the Courage to Call It Off   156

74. Should You Include Other Children in the Ceremony?   158

75. Let Go of "Non-Guest" Guilt   161

76. Consider Practical Ways to Trim Expenses   163

77. Learn to Compromise   165

78. Let Go of Pre-Wedding Conflict   166

79. Approve Even if They Disapprove   168

80. Treat In-Laws with Respect   170

81. Honor Your Mother and Father   172

82. Don't Complain to Him about His Mother   173

83. Handle Exes Graciously   175

84. Work with Your Coworkers   177

85. Be a Little Selfish with Your Time   179

86. Bid Farewell to Your Old Lifestyle   181

87. Embrace the Changes Ahead   182

88. Defend the "Sacred Week" of the Ceremony   184

89. Survive the "Day of" Emergencies   186

90. Prepare a Bridal Emergency Kit   188

91. Avoid Panic with Practice   190

92. Relax for the Rehearsal Dinner   192

93. "It's in God's Hands Now"   194

94. Revel in Pure Bliss   196

95. Conquer Stage Fright   197

96. There Is No Such Thing as a Flawless Wedding   199

97. Dance the Night Away   201

98. Make Your Escape   203

99. Conquer Wedding-Night Jitters   205

100. Embrace the Femininity of Your New Role   207

Foreword

Iasked a room full of people (mostly women) to tell me what their most stressful experience had been (not including life-or-death or truly serious events). An overwhelming percentage claimed that their wedding was at or near the top of the list. This was equally as true for women as they looked back on their weddings, as it was for women who were currently planning the big event. It was also true whether the wedding itself was large, or even relatively small.

Personally, I've known a huge number of people who have been married, and I can honestly say that most of them did indeed experience the event — especially the planning it — with a tremendous amount of stress. It's easy to see why. Your wedding is one of the most important events of your lifetime. It's one of the few celebrations when many, or even most, of the people you love and care about come together to celebrate — you. Naturally, you want everything to be perfect! You're justifiably a bit nervous.

Like many men, I lucked out during my own wedding. Kris and her mom, Patricia, did everything. All I had to do was to show up! I do remember, however, and have a great deal of respect and gratitude for the enormous amount of preparation that went into our big day. There were literally hundreds of details to attend to and take care of in the weeks preceding the wedding. As Kris read through this book, she said to me, "I would have loved to have read this before our wedding."

The editors of Don't Sweat Press have done a superb job in creating this guide to taking some of the stress out of a wedding. While there are many fine books on planning weddings, I've never seen one quite like this. Instead of focusing on the "how to's," this book is primarily geared toward helping you keep your perspective so that you can have the best possible overall experience.

When all is said and done, and the excitement of the day is over, it would be so nice to be able to look back and remember that you really enjoyed the entire experience. To me, that's the beauty of this particular book. By helping you focus on what's truly important, it encourages you to enjoy every step of the way. As you are able to stay more relaxed, the others involved in the wedding will pick up on your sense of calm as well.

Whether you're planning your own wedding or helping someone with theirs, this book can be very helpful and reassuring. It is filled with simple tips and reminders that can help make the difference between stress and ease. I hope it helps to make that special day even more special.

Richard Carlson

THE DON'T SWEAT GUIDE
FOR WEDDINGS

1.

Make a Date with Your Fiancé

Congratulations and best wishes! The question has been asked and answered. You are officially engaged to be married—which is why everyone keeps asking you: When and where?

Nailing down the initial points may seem like a daunting task. There are so many choices—and so many things to consider. We all know couples that have talked about getting married for years, but have yet to follow through on the act.

The hardest part of planning a wedding is, simply, getting started. Then again, if done correctly, the best part of planning a wedding is getting started.

Why not do it right? Ask your beloved on a date. Invite him to a candlelit dinner at your home. Set the scene with soothing music and lighting. Order in (or pre-cook) something savory in which to indulge yourselves. Don't forget about dessert, since your mission is to stay at the table until you have fully discussed the wedding.

Before supper, turn off your cell phones and shoo away all roommates. Sit down with a bottle of wine and your notepad.

Allow yourselves to fantasize. Ask your mate to picture his perfect wedding and describe it to you. Who are the people that he envisions around him? What is the setting? How are you dressed? Now you do the same.

Write these images down. Do you want a white-gown march down the aisle of a cathedral? Or an intimate gathering of friends on an exotic beach? Take time to dream. Explore the possibilities without regard to cost or logistics.

Once you have determined the moods and styles that are important to you, and perhaps compromised on your choices, you are ready to get down to business.

2.

Get a Grip — Start with the Basics

Developing an idea into an event is simply a matter of answering the basic questions of who, what, when, where, and how. With your wish lists in hand, each of you should consider the following issues.

Who are the people that you most want to be included in — and invited to witness — your union. Jot these people down, and add up the numbers for a rough estimate of guests.

With your major players in mind, look at the geographical logistics of *where* you want to hold your ceremony. Remember that it is your wedding day, and you will be doing most of the work. Plan the location around your convenience, then that of your families, and then that of your other guests.

When to hold your wedding is the next important decision. Although summer months tend to be the most popular due to weather conditions being more favorable for both outdoor events and travel, off-peak festivities can equal better availability and costs.

Be sure to think about any seasonal conflicts that may arise. Professional commitments, religious restrictions, and holidays should all be considered. One year is an ideal amount of time to plan ahead. Six months is adequate. Anything less than that can be made to work. If you have the option, however, give yourself more time rather than less.

Refer back to your fantasy weddings. With a rough size, date, and location in mind, take a look at what *type* of ceremony best matches your other priorities. Draw up a list of suggested places to hold your ceremony and your celebration.

With the general concepts in mind, decide *how* to implement your plan. Who is going to be responsible for which parts of the wedding? When is the best time to schedule visits with these people so that both of you can review your options?

Take a few minutes to touch upon the details. What types of food would you like to serve? What is your musical preference? How many bridesmaids and groomsmen should you have? And, most important, what type of honeymoon do you want? By capturing the basics, you have begun to plan your wedding.

3.

Come to Terms with
Religious Differences

As interdenominational unions become more popular, conventional weddings have become more complicated. But before the bride and groom even discuss their wedding plans, they should have an open talk about the role of spirituality in both their wedding ceremony and in their upcoming life together.

An understanding and respect for each other's spiritual stance is essential from the beginning of any new life together. The issue of religion takes on a greater magnitude when the spouses-to-be are of different persuasions. In this case, it is vital that the partners examine their own spirituality and discuss what is important to them. They may find it helpful to explain the teachings of their faith to each other. Each will want to decide which religious practices they want to continue. And this is the time to examine how you wish to raise any future children.

Blended beliefs are not uncommon these days, and can work very well. Many families combine their religious customs. If you and your intended disagree on what rituals to include in your wedding ceremony, you may find it helpful to locate an interfaith member of the clergy who will work with the two of you to design your own. Or you may opt to have two clergy members at your ceremony—one to represent each of your respective houses of worship.

Don't let any minor disagreements about your faith become major barriers to your wedding. The important thing is that both of your beliefs are respected at the ceremony and in your lives together.

4.

Give Yourself the Gift
of Backup Planning

With our busy schedules and hectic lifestyles, backup planning has become a necessity. This is an absolute must for wedding plans. It is especially important in the early planning stages, when the details are being worked out.

Once the major decisions have been made, write a second list of optional plans. Among other things, this may include an alternate date, place of ceremony (if possible), location of the reception, style of reception, and honeymoon destination.

Remember that it is much easier to explore two paths simultaneously than to run in one direction until you hit a wall and need to backtrack. Perhaps the music you've chosen is more expensive than you planned for—an alternate location might be a way to cut down on expenses and still be happy. Or perhaps the caterer you've chosen isn't free on a certain date—it is helpful if you keep your early scheduling more flexible.

Being aware of what you can and can't change will save you time and energy throughout the planning process. Explore all of your alternatives with your vendors during your initial conversations. That way, as the details come into focus, you will find yourself with more options rather than less.

5.

Play the Numbers Game

The rulebooks that prohibit a second-time bride from holding a traditional wedding have gathered a lot of dust by now. Today's woman may celebrate her nuptials in any way she wishes, regardless of how many trips she has made down the aisle.

Still, brides being remarried often prefer a lower-key celebration than their first. Most likely, they have already acted out their fairy-tale visions and did what was expected of them the last time around. They may have also used up any outside wedding funds that were previously available to them.

This means that second-time brides are often on their own for their subsequent unions—and it allows for a delicious freedom. Festivities unhindered by conventional requirements can be a lot more fun (and a lot less expensive) to plan.

Additionally, everyone is more understanding. Your friends won't mind if you choose to recite your vows in an out-of-the-way place and only invite your closest family members. They will also be thrilled if you decide to turn the event into a less formal atmosphere for as many people as you know.

If this marriage is not your first, enjoy the freedoms that you are afforded on your wedding day. Have a formal dinner party if you like. Celebrate with a theme wedding. Or even plan a small gathering of friends on the beach.

Remember that there aren't many rules for a second ceremony. One of the few is just to create a loving day that you and your groom will both remember.

6.

Share the News

Choosing a date and place for a wedding makes most couples want to shout this blissful news from the rooftops. However, before publicly announcing the details of your nuptials, be sure to run them past your closest friends and family members. Think of the loved ones that you couldn't bear to miss your union, and give them a call. Sort through any dates that would be impossible for them to be able to attend your wedding.

Additionally, after a few days of digesting your own plans, you and your mate may decide that what sounded like a good idea at the time isn't practical, romantic, or appealing to you anymore.

During this initial process, however, it is important for the couple to be firm in their decisions and not be swayed to change their date or location for the mere convenience of one guest or another. Remember that your plans will be inconvenient for *someone*, so make sure that you are aware of your priorities.

Once you and your betrothed have cleared the major dates with your loved ones, leak the rest of the details only after they are confirmed. Remember that it is far easier to give everyone the right information once than to tell half the people the wrong information two or three times.

7.

Take Pride in
Your Engagement Ring

It's a beautiful setting. The stone is brilliant in the light. This engagement ring is — well, perhaps, not what you expected.

While some brides are fortunate enough to be included in their engagement ring selection, many others can be surprised with jewelry already purchased by their intended mates. This can be a good or not-so-good thing.

Any woman who finds herself reluctant to wave her shiny new bauble under the noses of her friends should ask herself exactly what she was hoping for and why she is not pleased with the selection. It may be that the jewelry is simply not suited to your individual fashion style. Perhaps it is too large and looks gaudy on your slender finger. Or it might remind you of the one your partner gave to his ex-wife. If you believe that you would be satisfied with another ring in the same price range, an open discussion is in order. Reassure him that you greatly appreciate his efforts, but since you plan to wear this ring forever, you would be happier with one that better suits your individual tastes.

On the other hand, there are some women who find that they are not quite thrilled with the value of the jewelry itself. If the ring is an heirloom, or your husband-to-be has limited funds, it may be wise to try to live with the ring for the moment. You can always request another ring for your three- or five-year anniversary gift.

If, however, you find yourself growing resentful over the issue, it is time to take very tactful action. With a little tact, everyone can be happy—including your jeweler.

8.

Your Wedding Is Your Priority

Regardless of whether you are holding a traditional service for a thousand people or a small backyard ceremony for family only, every wedding is a special event. There will be many elements of planning that require careful attention over the next few weeks and months. Remember that your ceremony, honeymoon, and start of a new family life are your top priorities during this time.

Yes, other obligations will crop up. And everyone needs time with friends. But before you commit to any extracurricular activities, either professional or social, be sure to consult your bridal to-do list first. Then evaluate whether or not the event is truly worth putting ahead of your own priorities.

Recognize your wedding day as the significant event that it is. Then dedicate both your mental and physical energies to the cause. After all, how many weddings are you planning to have? And after all of these years of dreaming about the event, isn't it worth your full attention now to plan it?

9.

Explore Theme Weddings

Recently, theme weddings have gotten a bad rap. Even though each engaged couple should follow their hearts when it comes to their nuptials, theme weddings often are simply not the type of romantic ceremony that most of us imagine.

However, a theme wedding can be exactly the type of romantic ceremony that you and your betrothed envision. A focused event can be based on where the two of you met; a shared passion; or even a long-harbored dream. Weaving a common thread between the elements can also be a great way to exchange creative energy for traditional expenses.

Perhaps you work together, or share a passion for a particular hobby. Setting your wedding against a backdrop of the things that you love to share can be exhilarating and declare to the world that this is how you plan to spend your life: following your hearts together.

An occasion with character can be a lot of fun to plan and orchestrate. It will be an event to remember. And you may still incorporate any conventional wedding elements that you choose.

10.

Have the Courage to Break Tradition

I f every generation continued to hold on to every wedding tradition, certain cultures would still have engaged couples tying themselves together during their ceremonies. Other groups would shave the bride's head in preparation for her big day. And there are a lot of men out there who would never even get a glimpse of their intended partners until after the vows were exchanged.

Many of these customs have faded away. Others have evolved into modern tradition. For example, it is believed that the tossing of the bouquet and the garter belt actually started as a self-defense maneuver to keep fourteenth-century European wedding guests from ripping off pieces of the bride's gown, which were considered to be good luck.

Today, some women think of the bouquet toss as a fun event, while others believe that it is in bad taste to "bequeath the next set of nuptials" to the woman who can grab the flowers the quickest. Other women dislike having a sea of rice or birdseed stuck in their hair. And many prefer to eat the wedding cake rather than to wear it.

If you are not comfortable with a particular ritualistic tradition, you should dismiss it, by all means. This includes family customs, as well. You and yours-to-be are under no obligation to marry in the same church or synagogue where your parents and grandparents married. Those were their weddings; this is yours.

Although traditions may provide us with comforting ties to our cultural histories, they are traditions—not laws. As such, they may be observed or omitted, depending on our own personal preferences.

11.

Embrace New Tradition

Why not incorporate the special moments of your life with your fiancé into the celebration of your love? These little touches could become treasured moments for years to come.

Some couples save a case of the wine served at their wedding to celebrate their special occasions in the months and years to come. Others freeze a part of their wedding cake and enjoy it on their first anniversary.

You can also include traditional elements from your past. Perhaps you and your betrothed have made a habit of celebrating special events with cappuccino and cheesecake. This could make an excellent alternative to serving a conventional wedding cake. Do the two of you make it a point to pull over to the side of the road to pick wildflowers? Then what could make better centerpieces than daisies and daffodils?

You may even want to change a standard custom into one of your own. When one bride ordered her flowers, she had five separate bouquets gathered into one, held in place with a single ribbon, which she carried down the aisle. Instead of tossing the creation at her reception, she untied the ribbon and handed each of her bridesmaids their own bouquets. Every one of them copied her bouquet trend in their own weddings, and a new tradition was born.

After all, traditions are simply good ideas that get repeated. So why not come up with a few of your own to personalize your wedding day and the beginning of your new life with your husband?

12.

Show Your Personality

Do you and your mate share a special interest that you feel defines you? It may be a worthy task to add this passionate aspect of yourselves to your union. This does not necessarily mean that you need to recite your vows while hiking up Mount Everest, or that you must scuttle down the aisle wearing scuba gear. There are many ways to incorporate a unique characteristic into a traditional ceremony.

Perhaps you and your fiancé met at work. Is there anything about your workplace that is special or exciting that could be incorporated into your day? Are you and your intended singers or amateur musicians? Why not personalize your reception with your own music? Even small details can leave people with a lasting impression of your ceremony. Give your guests a souvenir from your wedding that says something personal about you, or that plays up your honeymoon destination.

If you add an aspect of your personality to your wedding, you may still enjoy a conventional ceremony. Yet you will give your guests something special with which to remember your day.

13.

Consider Hiring a Professional

Many brides-to-be assume that hiring a wedding consultant is beyond their means and pocketbooks. They believe that a coordinator is a luxury, used only by the rich and famous for elaborate, perfectly planned affairs.

The truth of the matter is that most professional wedding planners have a menu of timesaving services. Their assistance can range from negotiating the basics to hand-holding through the event itself. While the services can cost anywhere from a few hundred to a few thousand dollars, a planner may actually save you money in the end.

Most professionals work within a limited geographical area. They have relationships with local vendors. They know who is reliable and how their prices compare. Consultants bring repeat business to facilities and suppliers, and are often privy to certain discounts. They are practiced in the fine art of negotiation, and may even suggest options that you and your groom hadn't considered.

The real advantage of hiring a wedding planner, however, is the time that he or she will save you. With the average ceremony and reception requiring 250 hours of planning, it may be worth your while to hire someone to do the legwork and handle some details. This is especially true if you have limited time to prepare, or if you are planning a long-distance event.

Additionally, having a professional around on the day of your ceremony can be invaluable. That is where their talents of emergency management and running interference with difficult family members can shine. While many brides still prefer the old "roll up your sleeves and dig in" method of wedding planning, hiring a professional is certainly worth a consideration.

14.

Do You Prefer a
Child-Free Wedding?

Whether or not to include children on the guest list can be a monumental decision that should be discussed in the early planning stages. Some couples feel that these small guests bring a certain sense of family to the celebration. Others believe that an elegant wedding is an adults-only occasion.

Obviously, a degree of common sense is required in this choice. For example, if children are included in the wedding ritual, they can hardly be excluded from the reception. And one cannot invite certain children but not others (unless you employ an age limit).

However you and your mate choose to handle this issue is strictly up to you. The important thing is that you prepare for either decision. For a child-filled festivity, you may want to consider hiring a baby-sitter to watch the youngsters during the ceremony (perhaps even in a separate room). Ask someone to organize a children's table at the reception, complete with crayons, paper, and games. Also be sure to check with your hall about high chair availability, and to check with your caterer about kids' meals. In general, both the children and your budget will be happier if the kids' plates contain hot dogs rather than roast beef.

To ensure a kid-free event, make sure that you and your fiancé stand firm in your decision, and then spread the word among your close friends and relatives. Be prepared to call anyone who asks about children to gently explain your stance. For your out-of-town guests who plan to tow along their young children, it may be helpful if you contact a local baby-sitter or nanny service to request references and pass this information along.

The choice is yours: kids or no kids. Whichever way you prefer to handle the issue, a little planning in the beginning may save a lot of chaos in the end.

15.

Your Wedding Organizer

Details, details, and more details can drive any sane person crazy. A portable organizer to record all wedding information is an indispensable investment for every bride-to-be. In fact, according to a survey by *Brides* magazine, nearly 20 percent of 2,700 engaged women claimed that they would rather lose their wallets than their wedding planners.

Whether you choose to carry a simple notebook or a formal planning guide, an organizer is your most potent weapon against chaos. The advantage of purchasing a printed wedding guide is that it may contain checklists and agendas. Although you will probably need to customize both according to your situation, they can be invaluable memory-joggers.

Be sure to record all of the names, phone numbers, and details pertinent to your planning in this book as you go along. This includes the friends who are helping you, your reception hall manager, and the person who is building your trellis. For business contacts, it is also helpful to write down assistants' names and the companies hours of operation.

If you find yourself digging through your purse for the little slip of paper with the florist's phone number, it is time to gather all of your information and write it down in one place where you always have it at your fingertips—in your wedding organizer. Just try not to lose it.

16.

Treat Your Wedding
Like a Business

There are appointments. There are contracts. There are a whole lot of phone calls. Many soon-to-be-brides feel that planning their weddings becomes a second job. And, indeed, some people do make a living by coordinating events. Here are some tips from professional event-planners to make your new job easier.

Treat your wedding like a separate business. What tools will you need to get this job done? Gather together a notepad, pens, and paperclips or a small stapler. Pick up several file folders, preferably with pockets for collected brochures and menus. Designate a space in your home, such as a section of a countertop or a small table, to store all of your planning information. Also specify a particular pocket of your briefcase or a separate shoulder bag to carry the files with you on appointments.

Make goals and give yourself deadlines. Stick to them. In your organizer, list your upcoming tasks and their projected completion dates. Don't try to accomplish everything at once. But do try to have all of your detail work finished and confirmed two weeks before the ceremony. If, along the way, you feel tempted to skip one of your deadlines, picture yourself explaining to your boss why you could not finish your work in time.

Individualize your strategy based on your own effectiveness. When is the best time of day for you to make appointments and phone calls? Plan your scheduling around these times, and make sure that your vendors know the best time and way to get in touch with you.

Create a strategy in advance. By doing this, the entire process will flow more smoothly through to the end.

17.

Appreciate Your Beloved
for Who He Is

There are, no doubt, many wonderful qualities about your sweetheart. That is why he is going to be your groom. But recognize that wedding planning may not be one of them.

For better or worse, women today still shoulder the bulk of the organizing for weddings. We have been raised with bridal enthusiasm, whereas usually our men have been taught to stay out of our way.

To involve your man in the project, take a look at his special talents and abilities. Ask him to pitch in where he is most capable. For instance, a wine connoisseur will enjoy organizing the menu and the bar. Are you marrying a gifted gardener? Why not ask him to organize the floral decorations or trellis? Does your intended fancy himself to be a world traveler? You have your honeymoon planner.

If your beloved feels valuable, he will also feel more enthusiastic about the entire project. Just remember that handing over a task means just that—keeping your hands off of it. While both partners should review the major decisions of any wedding issues, the details of his tasks should be his to plan.

Ask for your man's help where he is the best suited, and then step back and respect his judgment. He is, after all, the expert in that field. Isn't that one of the reasons that you fell in love with him in the first place?

18.

Learn to Say Yes

Some brides look absolutely radiant on their wedding day—and other brides look just plain exhausted. Both groups of women smiled politely and said thank you when their friends and relatives offered to help with wedding plans. The rested brides actually took their relatives and friends up on such offers. The tired-looking women tried to do it all themselves.

As women, we can still hold on to that outdated myth of the wonder woman. We think we can do everything, do it all at once, and do it well without any assistance. Besides, we don't want to *impose* on anyone. However, the best thing a busy bride can do is learn to say yes to any offers of assistance.

Historically, marriages were a communal celebration. All of the local women rejoiced in preparing a feast to signify the future growth and abundance of their village or tribe. While our society has outgrown many ancient traditions, we sometimes forget that weddings still possess a sense of community spirit. People want to be involved in the occasion and celebrate your joy with you.

This can be a win-win situation for everyone. Remember that everyone likes to feel needed. And your friends want you to achieve your main objective: to enjoy your day. When they offer to help, it comes from the heart. So smile; say thank you; and then say yes!

19.

Get Help for
the Honeymoon

In ancient times, the honeymoon simply meant the couple's initial weeks together. "Honey" referred to mead—a love and fertility drink of the Romans made from honey, which was an essential part of the couple's celebration. "Moon" referred to the lunar cycle, or what we call a "month." It was the custom of several cultures to spend this time at the groom's mother's house.

At present, a honeymoon is a chance to escape the world while you spend your first few glorious days together as husband and wife. Unless you already have specific plans underway, you and your fiancé will need to decide what type of trip that you want to take and where to go. Will it be an adventure? A sightseeing tour? Or a trip to somewhere isolated and romantic?

Next, consult your budget. After reviewing the numbers, some couples choose to take a short holiday right after their ceremony, while scheduling a dream trip for their upcoming future. This gives them a chance to catch up on their agendas outside of the wedding plans and their checkbooks. Other newlyweds desire just a few relaxing nights together without the stress of major travel plans. To them, a nearby resort town for the weekend is their perfect getaway. Still other couples want to capture the adrenaline-packed thrills of their wedding festivities and whisk that excitement straight to an exotic island. They are typically boarding a flight by the time the band is playing its final number.

Whatever type of trip you have in mind, your first call should be for some honeymoon help. Trying to plan "the event after the event" at the same time you are planning "the event" can be overwhelming. Something will inevitably end up getting shortchanged—and it is usually the honeymoon plan.

If you are staying local, ask a responsible friend to order some maps and brochures from the area. (Fathers tend to be good at this kind of thing.) Even for smaller trips, it may be worthwhile to consult a travel agent.

For larger trips, a professional is invaluable. An agent can suggest options that you may not have considered, and simultaneously give you the best rates for each. This can shave hours off your honeymoon research time and save days of phone calls making reservations. Good travel agents may even arrange for a bottle of champagne to be sent to your room. And they will never, ever suggest that you spend the first few nights at your new mother-in-law's house.

20.

Celebrate Your Choice
of Bridesmaids

When choosing our bridesmaids, we may feel as though we have one of two options—we can appoint fifty of our closest friends, or we can walk solo down the red carpet.

We are not obligated, of course, to have any bride's or groom's attendants. In very small weddings, it is often the case to have none —or merely one—of each. This does generally simplify the decision process.

But most of us do have a few of our friends stand up for us. Large ceremonies may even have up to a dozen maids. Choosing the number of attendants is, of course, initially dependent on the overall size of your guest list. Based on your own preferences, there is no right or wrong number. However, there may be some difficult decisions.

You will probably want to take a look at your immediate family first. Your sisters and brothers have been with you since childhood and will (hopefully) always be part of your future. Although there may be a stray sibling or two that you only speak to at holiday functions, family members are often key parts of our lives and the milestones that we reach.

Longtime friends also deserve special consideration. After all, what would a celebration be if it didn't include our college roommates whom we've called every Tuesday for the last ten years?

Logistics may also play a part in your decision. Perhaps the person whom you most want to stand up for you cannot, because of geographic or financial constraints. In these cases, it helps to evaluate what responsibilities your attendants will have and whether your loved ones can meet them. Many times, the answer is no, and in that case, a truthful explanation usually diffuses any bad feelings. Often those who know that they cannot perform as you would like them to are relieved to give up that responsibility.

Finally, do not forget how important your groom's family is in your union. Your two sisters and childhood friend may pair up beautifully with your husband-to-be's three brothers. But what about his sister? One bride found her solution by appointing both a maid and a matron of honor. She had them both escorted by the best man. Everyone, including the bride, was happy. As an added bonus, she had twice the help to organize her wedding ceremony.

21.

Honor Those Whom You Cherish

While organizing your wedding, you may find that there are certain people, near and dear to you and your future groom, on whom you wish to bestow a special honor during your ceremony. There are many ways to do this.

The most popular method of including special others is to have them sing a song or recite a verse during your ceremony. Some brides invite a special man to help escort them down the aisle (as long as dad doesn't mind). Other couples ask their officiators to make a statement directly to family members.

The reception is full of opportunities to recognize loved ones. Why not ask someone to make a special toast after the best man recites his? You could display wedding photos of your parents and grandparents at the sign-in table. Or arrange for the deejay to spin a song dedicated to a particular couple that has guided you and your husband-to-be. Ask them to be the first dancers for that song, and then join the dance floor after a few moments.

Take a moment to appreciate those with whom you have a special relationship. It will not only enrich their experience of your wedding; it will also enrich yours.

22.

Make Peace
with Your Guest List

O nce the couple has decided on the number of guests they *can* invite, the next big question becomes *whom* to invite. They draw up a list. They change it two or three times. Then they come up with the names of new guests they *should* invite nearly every day until the big event. It may be helpful to reference the following rules of thumb when pounding out your guest list.

Remember your numbers. For large weddings, the philosophy is: "When in doubt, send an invitation out." Smaller weddings subscribe to the opposite. "If you're unsure, skip the invitation."

Do not invite too many. Couples often invite more people than they can accommodate on the assumption that a lot of potential guests will not be able to attend. In general, more people will RSVP than you expect. The safest way to handle vacancies is to send out your invitations well in advance. Call the guests that you've not heard back from. Only after your "A-list" has been confirmed can you comfortably allocate the available spaces to new in

Keep control of your guest list. Start by designat
number of slots to your parents and your in-laws. Be
both know which family members and friends are on t
(to avoid duplicates) and that the other spaces already have backup
names. The closer you get to your wedding date, the more pressure
you may be under to add your mother's hairdresser or your father's
dentist to the list. This is the time that you will need to gently but
firmly stick to your guns.

Steer away from playing favorites. You may not want a particular
family member to attend your nuptials. But if you invite the rest of
that person's immediate family, the absence will be quite conspicuous
and may not reflect well on you. Even if you have a long-standing
feud with someone, it may be to your advantage to send an
invitation. Let him decline if he wants to, but you may be surprised
when he decides to attend. Weddings can be a wonderful time to
bridge troubled waters. And what about the potentially troublesome
guest? The one who is always loud or gets a little too rowdy at
gatherings? While it boils down to a judgment call between you and
your husband, it may help to remember the first rule of thumb. In a
large ceremony, invite the maybes. In a smaller union, where they
can be more disruptive, skip the invitation.

Ultimately, you and your fiancé are free to decide whom you do
and do not want at your wedding. But remembering these
guidelines may help you to polish your list to a shine.

23.

Handle Coworkers
and Acquaintances with Grace

One of your trickiest wedding tasks can be to decide which coworkers and acquaintances to invite. After all, you may have been chatting about your wedding plans with your office mates, hairdresser, and yoga buddies for two months. And now you realize that your guest list is not large enough to accommodate all of them.

There are three main considerations to weigh when dealing with coworkers. What is the size of your wedding? What is the size of your company or department? And who are the employees that you already intend to invite?

If you are having a small wedding and happen to work with one or two of your best friends, there is nothing wrong with only inviting a couple of people from the office. On the other hand, if you are having a mid- to large-sized wedding and have already invited four of your seven coworkers, you may need to extend invitations to the rest of the group to avoid hurt feelings.

The same applies equally to acquaintances. Inviting two of your three bridge partners is, obviously, not in good taste. However, if you have become chummy with one in particular, and the others are aware of your relationship, then that one invitation should not be an issue.

For both sets of people, it is essential to examine the types of relationships that you have with these individuals. Do you spend any leisure time with your office mates, or only see them during the day? Do you intend to stay at your company, or leave at the first opportunity? Are your social groups ongoing, or a set length of time, as in, for example, a cooking class? In other words, will these people continue to play a role in your life once you have moved on?

It may be uncomfortable, at first, to omit your coworkers from your wedding—or to invite everyone, including the office gossip whom you dislike. But a little diplomacy in the planning stages of your guest list may save you money and strife in the end—both of which you will be happy about when you return from your honeymoon.

24.

Forgo the
Wedding Announcements

All of those numerous albums of sample wedding invitations also include matching announcements. Many printers are quite eager to point out the benefits of these additional orders. "By sending an announcement to those people whom you cannot invite," the printer may say, "they won't feel bad about not getting an invitation."

In years past, this may have been true. Since the announcement carries no obligation of a gift or an invitation, it was intended for people close enough to you to be informed of your marriage but not close enough to actually be involved in the celebration.

Today, however, the announcement has become nearly obsolete, and gone with it is the understanding of what it actually means. Unless a couple has eloped, or announcements are a strong family tradition, most modern couples can easily skip the time, cost, and energy of sending out these printed cards.

Other written notices of your nuptials could be more contemporary. An announcement in your church bulletin, for example, may be welcomed and, in some religions, actually required. Sending an engagement notification to the local newspaper is a widely observed custom that you may or may not wish to follow.

Traditionally, the mother of the bride handled the notices to the newspaper, as did the mother of the groom if he was from a different town. In our mobile society, it may be easier to designate a friend to do the honors. Simply hand her an invitation (or the details, including the parents' names). Optionally, you can give her a photo of you or one of you and your groom-to-be. The photo does not need to be professional—do not expect it to be returned.

By skipping the printed announcements and handing off media announcements, many brides can breathe easier. Now there is one less thing that requires their attention.

25.

Find the Perfect Dress

O ne of the bride's most exciting tasks is to choose her wedding gown. Many of us start to fantasize about what we will wear on the day that we say "I do" at the same moment that we say "Yes, I will."

Searching for that perfect gown to bring your childhood images to life is a highly charged and extremely personal experience. First, remember that your wedding is actually a projection of your own bridal illusion. If it weren't, we would all save ourselves the trouble and expense of holding a ceremony and simply bop down to the local justice of the peace. The illusion that you are creating is brought into focus by the style of ceremony that you are holding. And it is defined by the costume that you wear.

With a mental image in mind, you can start to browse through magazines, bridal shops and shows, or department stores for the gowns that best match your ceremonial style and personal tastes. Once you have a clear idea of what illusion you want to portray, it is time to get serious about purchasing your dream dress.

To keep your search simple, you need to take two essential pieces of equipment with you: an honest friend and a Polaroid camera. Have your friend stand back about ten feet and take a photo of each dress that you try on (and there will be many). That way, as you go from store to store, and again at the end of the evening, when all of the seas of fabric are flowing together in your mind, you will have a clear record to capture and compare each gown.

You may want to ditch tradition and wear a snazzy suit—or an antique dress, or your mom's gown. Whatever you decide, make sure that the dress is what you want—not what you've been pressured into thinking you have to wear.

When you find the dress that you want and place an order, be sure to check out the accessories that the shops offer. Do not leave these until the last minute. The accessories, like the gown and the ceremony itself, are all part of the same picture.

26.
Don't Stress over
Writing Your Vows

Proclaiming your love to your betrothed in front of witnesses can be quite a touching moment. Many couples choose to forgo the conventional "I do's" in favor of more personal nuptials. Capturing those wedding words, however, can be tricky. More than one bride has started to pen her vows months in advance and finished the deed in a scribble on the drive to the altar. On the days in between, the shadow of the task became another source of her to-do list anxiety.

So if you are planning to write your own vows, get rid of that anxiety right now. When is the *first* opportunity that you have to schedule a half-hour—just thirty minutes—of quiet time? Schedule that time into your agenda.

By writing out a set of vows now, you have the option of rewriting the vows later if you are struck by sudden inspiration. Just remember that waiting for sudden inspiration is akin to watching the proverbial pot boil—especially when you expect that inspiration to tell you the perfect thing to say.

The most important consideration is the length of your solo. While a long soliloquy may seem romantic in the silence of your kitchen, you may not feel comfortable making a drawn-out speech in front of a crowd.

Start by jotting down a few phrases that remind you of your love for your fiancé. Perhaps they are lines from "your" song, a poem, a romantic movie, or even a card. Just record whatever comes to mind.

Next, write down your answers to the following questions: Why do you love him? What do you feel you are promising him by becoming his wife? What is he giving to you by becoming your husband? What does this marriage mean to you? How do you envision your future together?

Read over your thoughts. Take the strongest phrases and points, and loosely string them together into one to two paragraphs. Do not worry if they don't make sense. This is not a speech; these are simply words from your heart.

Speak them out loud two or three times. If you can picture yourself reciting these vows in front of your friends and family, script them onto an index card. This is your cheat sheet, should you need it. Now, you at least have a set of vows written, and you can cross "Write wedding vows" off of your to-do list.

27.

The Wedding Rings

There are many legends laying claim to the origin of the wedding ring, and no single account is any more plausible than the next. Some anthropologists believe that the band is a symbol of the shackles used during the "marriage by capture" days. Others attribute the custom to the ancient Middle East, where rings were used as a form of currency. And there are historical accounts that state that the piece of jewelry was used as a talisman to ward off evil spirits in search of a new bride's soul.

Throughout the ages, wedding bands have been constructed of many different metals and taken on several forms. It is unclear when, exactly, that gold came to symbolize everlasting love and devotion. But it *is* known that the exchange of rings by both spouses has only become popular within the last century.

The fact that giving a man a wedding band is a fairly new tradition may be the reason why we ladies haven't yet mastered this technique. Quite often, we race off to our favorite jeweler and plunk down a deposit on a stunning pair of matching, diamond-etched beauties without even considering our mate's preference in the matter. It's an easy mistake to make. After all, if you love the rings, then he'll love them, right?

Perhaps. But it is just as possible that he may have his own design in mind. Maybe he prefers a silver band, reminiscent of his father's ring from his mother. He may want an elaborate ring to match the elegant suits he wears to the office. More often than not, men request something thin and simple that won't become a hindrance (or a danger) when they're working with their hands.

Just be sure to talk to your fiancé before you talk to your jeweler. If the wedding band suits your betrothed in the beginning, you won't find it sitting on top of the dresser down the road.

28.

Come to Terms with
the Prenuptials

Every marriage license is a contract. It is an agreement between you, your betrothed, and the government. Within the government, you gain certain rights and obligations, which are pretty standard.

Your rights and obligations to each other are quite different. They are based on the expectations that you have of each other. It is important to have an understanding of what those expectations are.

Sometimes, people will write these expectations down on paper. "You agree to provide this, and I agree to provide that." When substantial amounts of money are at stake, it is not uncommon for attorneys to draw up documentation designating who is entitled to what—before, during, and, if need be, after the marriage.

The romantics among us believe that these prenuptial agreements are a negative sign that dictates duties and predicts the end of a beautiful love. The more practical folks say that "prenups" are merely a way to avoid marital discourse during (and if need be, after) the relationship.

Whether your prenuptial agreement is certified by the courts or merely a quiet understanding of your upcoming lives together, make sure that there is an understanding of what you are signing up for. One of the most common complaints among new wives, for instance, is the division of housework. Some women are convinced that by saying words "I do," a man's memory of how to turn on the washing machine or unload the dishwasher is automatically erased.

If this is your betrothed's expectation of married life, you will most certainly want to know about it in advance. Similarly, if you plan to quit your job and take care of the house, you need to inform him of his expected role as the sole provider.

Other issues to address may be who contributes what funds to the household; who is responsible for cooking and cleaning up; and who will primarily raise the children. Each of you has an image of what to expect from the other, based on your own upbringing and your own lifestyles. It is important to talk these expectations through and gain a clear understanding of what your nuptial agreement includes.

29.

The Name Change

Changing your name can be a scary task. After all, you've probably been the same person all of your life. Now, you may suddenly have a different title and a new name. It may make you feel as though you are trading one identity for another.

In a way, you are. You are exchanging your single identity for the shared identity of couplehood. As if that doesn't sound daunting enough, you may also be swapping your name to solidify the deal.

In the United States, it is still traditional for a wife to replace her surname with her husband's. Although this can cause temporary disruption (and a lot of paperwork), it can help to avoid future confusion with legal forms and your future children. But it may also feel confining to some. For business executives who rely on their reputations, or artists who are known by their names, a name change may be a distinct disadvantage.

There are several other options available. It is perfectly acceptable for today's wedded woman to retain her maiden name, which may help her to maintain her individuality and simplify her professional life. That decision, however, may also become a source of frustration if she finds herself continuously explaining the name discrepancy to banks, credit lenders, the government, insurance companies, and children's teachers. Some will request a copy of her wedding license before they allow the couple to conduct further business.

A relatively new way to handle the previous conflicts is for a woman to hyphenate her maiden name with her new husband's last name. Hyphenated names have found a moderate degree of success in today's society. It does achieve the objectives of maintaining one's identity while also consecrating the marriage. But such names can be long and confusing. They are often misfiled. And the question of what to name the children may still be an issue.

However you decide to handle the name change may take some initial adjustments. But remember that you will be using your name —whether it is the original or revised—for many years to come. You are the one who needs to be happy with it.

30.

Engage Yourself in a Party

It's a good guess that from the moment you walk into a room with a ring on your finger, people will know that you are engaged. Most of them will know to whom you are promised. It is perfectly acceptable to use word of mouth to announce your intentions. However, if your schedule allows, an engagement party is a great way to host your first event together as husband- and wife-to-be.

Many engagement festivities these days are hosted by the couple-to-be to celebrate their partnership. As long as everyone who is invited to the announcement party will also be invited to the wedding (unless you are planning to elope and the celebration is meant to replace a ceremony), there are no rules for holding an engagement event.

You may ask your friends to meet you at a particular restaurant for brunch or for cocktails. You may host a sit-down dinner party. Or you may simply stand up at a designated family event (such as a Thanksgiving meal) and announce your intentions.

If you do plan to invite a group of people for a special occasion, it is a good idea to have the details of your nuptials ironed out. At the very least, your friends and family will want to know what month and what city.

Guests should by no means be expected to bring gifts. This is, after all, the announcement of your engagement, and most of the attendees will be bringing you gifts for your wedding.

31.

Know Your Budget

According to recent statistics, today's standard American wedding —for an average of 186 guests—costs nearly $20,000. And that is after much whittling, weeding, and compromising.

If money is absolutely no object, then plan away. Most of us, however, do need to keep an eye on the bottom line. The simple reality is that regardless of your wedding-day fantasies, money does matter, and it will shape the direction of your plans.

First, list how much you think you can allocate to each category of your ceremony and celebration. A wedding planner may help you to compile this list. If you are organizing the affair on your own, it may be beneficial to contact a recently married friend or a few local restaurants for comparative prices in your area.

Although every wedding is different, here is an illustration of a traditional ceremony based on a budget close to $20,000.

Pre-wedding parties . . . . . $ 1,000
Clothing . . . . $ 2,000

Invitations	$ 300
Flowers	$ 1,000
Music	$ 1,000
Photography	$ 1,500
Rental hall	$ 2,000
Caterer	$ 4,000
Bar	$ 3,000
Decorations	$ 1,000
Cake	$ 500
Transportation	$ 600
Gifts	$ 400
Rings	$ 1,000
Officiator donations	$ 200
Tips	$ 500
Miscellaneous	$ 1,000

Although your dollar figures will likely be revised two, three, or forty times before your actual trek down the aisle, knowing your budget in advance will help steer you in the right direction from the initial planning stages. It will also keep you from running too far down the wrong path. After all, what good is a $15,000 designer wedding gown when you can only afford to wear it in front of twenty people at the local YMCA?

32.

Specify Your Funding

Once you have a dollar estimate of what your wedding may cost, consider the source of your funding. You may find that you and your fiancé are paying for a large portion of the ceremony. If this is the case, name the funds that you currently have available to you. Can you contribute from your savings accounts, or each put aside a certain amount from your salaries to prepare for the day?

Perhaps your mother and father have offered to pay for a small reception. Wonderful. Did they define "small"? What does their "paying for it" include? Your fiancé's family may have mentioned that they will take care of the rehearsal dinner and the honeymoon airline tickets. What did they have in mind? Is there a financial limit on what they can afford? While it is sometimes difficult to broach the subject of finances, especially with our parents, an open path of communication is necessary to avoid undue difficulties later in the planning stages.

Try sharing your plans with your folks. If you are thinking about having 200 people at the local country club, tell your parents. Then listen for feedback. It may be wise to advise them of the range in price between a pasta buffet and a served dinner, and also to let them know which you prefer.

Although you may be initially reluctant to discuss the money issues with your sponsors (even if you are underwriting the event yourselves), it will be far more comfortable in the long run to know your freedoms and limitations. Otherwise, you may encounter a potentially embarrassing situation.

33.

Be Flexible with Funds

A couple of generations ago, budgeting for a wedding may have been much easier. Back then, brides and grooms typically went straight from under their parents' roofs into their own home. Because of this, tradition called for each family to pay for certain aspects of the wedding.

Today, however, things are different. In many cases, our parents were (rightfully so) more concerned about putting money away for our education than our wedding ceremonies. They may have also already helped us to establish ourselves when we started our careers. And they may even have contributed to a wedding in our past.

Regardless of your situation, any funds that your families do offer toward your wedding are invaluable gifts—and must be treated as such. Remember that no one outside of you and your mate are obligated to fund a single penny of your celebration.

If your respective families do have the means and the desire to help you and your spouse-to-be finance part of your ceremony, here is an old-fashioned breakdown of family contributions.

Bride's Family:
Invitations
Bride's clothing and accessories
Florist
Music
Photography
Gifts to groom and bridesmaids
Groom's wedding ring
Hall and food

Groom's Family:
Marriage license
Groom's clothing and accessories
Bride's engagement ring
Bride's wedding ring
Rehearsal dinner
Gifts to bride and groomsmen
Clergy fees
Honeymoon expenses

When approaching your families, do not assume that they will foot the bill for any portion, much less the whole, of your wedding. But if a family member does offer to cover particular expenses, or to contribute a dollar figure for you to apply as you see fit, thank that person profusely. Appreciate their gift completely. Then plan your budget accordingly.

34.

List Your Priorities

You and your betrothed may have already jotted down the when, where, and how decisions of the wedding on one piece of paper. You should have an estimated budget sketched out on a second sheet. How do they compare? Many of us may find that there is a big difference in what we desire and what we can afford.

If this is the case, it's time to turn both lists facedown and start a third—your true priority list. That does not mean that you will need to give up your fantasy wedding. On the contrary, it is a way to purchase the wedding of your dreams with the dollars in your pocket.

What do you and your groom feel are the most important aspects of your wedding? Do you envision a lavish evening of imported champagne in crystal glasses? Or are you more concerned that the event can be attended by as many of your extended family members and friends as can make it? Some couples who are financing a substantial portion of both their wedding and their honeymoon may choose to hold a simpler ceremony in order to reserve their funds for a more elaborate trip.

Define the aspects of the wedding that are the most important to you as individuals. This is the first step in reconciling your ways with your means to create the ceremony that you truly want.

35.

Restructure Your Plans

There is a moment of truth for every bride in terms of financing the wedding. It simply boils down to wishes versus numbers. That doesn't mean that you can't have it all; it simply calls attention to the need for practicality. A little self-negotiation can go a long way.

One of the most obvious ways to slash your expenses is to reduce the number of guests. A small, intimate affair can have the same pizzazz as a larger crowd without the extra meals and glasses of wine. However, if it is more important to you that your entire family and all of your friends are with you to celebrate, then you may want to take another look at the style of wedding that you are planning.

A fairly painless way to match your priorities to your budget may be to change the timing of the affair. Is there a particular reason to hold the event in May? Unless you have ordered the invitations and made deposits on your professional services, it may behoove you to reschedule the affair for four months later, when the off-season will result in better rates at area hotels and discounted floral services. It may also give you more time to shop for that perfect wedding dress with the perfect price tag.

There are many ways to reconcile your matrimonial visions with your pocketbook. The important thing is to recognize what your priorities are and how they fit into your overall plan.

36.

Seek Creative Solutions

Combining your own desires with budget limitations and the expectations of others can require some creative thought. One bride had reevaluated the major issues of her ceremony and still found that her dream exceeded her dollars. By dreaming up some "what if" scenarios, she was able to find a solution that suited her style and allowed her to overcome her money obstacles.

Perhaps an elegant reception for 200 people is what you want. *What if* you opted for a buffet dinner, but dressed up the occasion by having waiters circulate tasty appetizers during a sophisticated cocktail party? *What if* you change your celebration to a brunch affair or a tea, which would give you the same service for a less expensive meal and time frame to rent the restaurant? The expense of an outdoor celebration at a country club could be cut in half if you ask, "What if" you hold the festivities at a friend's country home, rent the necessary equipment, and hire a caterer? A little "what if" brainstorming with a friend or group of friends could easily result in a creative solution for your budget problems.

37.

Keep Simplicity in Mind

How many of us have dreamt of this day since we were young girls? Your wedding is, after all, one of the most sacred rituals in your lifetime. It is natural to want to pursue the vivid details of our fantasies.

But chasing fantasies can be an exhausting task. While you certainly want to portray the image that you always envisioned, taking the time to perfect every detail will quickly replace your enthusiasm with exasperation. The same is true for keeping track of every penny in your budget. Oftentimes, if the service is a value worth the price, you should just pay the price.

Don't bog yourself down with the details. It is not uncommon for a fiancée to scour a dozen bridal shops in search of the "perfect" veil. Then, two weeks later, she'll return to the first shop she visited to order the first veil that she tried on. Keep simplicity in mind when shopping for your essentials. Your bridal shop will carry accessories—invitation samples—and restaurant menus. Why not pick up those items while you're there, instead of putting them on your to-do list for later?

Don't always follow the dollar. It may be a few cents cheaper to hunt through the discount shoe stores until you find white satin pumps, and then dye them yourself to match that antique-hued wedding gown. But if you can order matching shoes at the same time and place that you order your dress, it may be worth the money for all of the energy it would save you.

Combine services when it's appropriate. Ask your caterers if they offer wedding cake services. Try using the same restaurant or reception hall for several of the pre-wedding and wedding events. And while ordering your invitations, consider buying thank-you cards to write personal notes in for later.

If you let it, each aspect of the wedding plan can become a project in itself. Getting sidetracked in the beginning will only result in frustration when time is running short in the end. So recognize the easiest way to get the job done — and get it done right. Keep simplicity in mind.

38.

Be Sensitive to the
Feelings of Your Parents

Each family has a different set of circumstances and a varied amount of funds that they may or may not be able to contribute to your wedding. Again, any contribution is a gift, and needs to be respected as such.

Be sensitive to the needs and limitations of your families. Most parents strive to give their children the best that they can afford. And some parents may even bestow more than they can afford on their children. Keep your family's situation in mind before expecting or accepting any gift.

It is important to be aware of the feelings of the family that is unable to help fund the event to the degree that they would like. Be sure to keep them updated and ask their opinions so they don't feel left out of the planning process.

Be extra sensitive when one family can afford a more lavish gift than the other. For instance, perhaps the bride's parents are paying for the ceremony, and the groom's parents have offered to pick up the tab for the reception. There should be no discernable difference between the styles of the affairs.

If you and your groom have announced that you prefer to handle the costs of the wedding yourselves, and your parents still wish to contribute, try designating a particular item or event to the gracious families. Maybe your mother would like to donate the flowers and your father-in-law would consider hosting an engagement party. Or perhaps each wants to just contribute a certain amount of cash for you to designate as you please.

However you choose to handle family contributions, be sure to keep each family member and their circumstances in mind during the planning process. This way, you can avoid unintentionally hurting someone's feelings.

39.

More Specific Now,
Less Stressed Later

Caterers, photographers, florists, decorators, and banquet hall managers may offer so many choices that it is sometimes tempting to just write down the basics and leave the details for later. Unfortunately, this may also lead to a lot of stress later.

To save yourself unanswered questions and multiple phone calls, make it a point to list all of the items to be covered during your meetings with these potential vendors. While you have the time to sit down with them, take a few extra minutes to cover all of the details that might come up later.

The first bit of ground to cover is their availability for the date (and alternate dates) of your planned event. In fact, it is worth the effort to ask about this in your initial phone calls when setting up appointments to interview them. During your interviews, be sure to ask about your first choices (dates, locations, and so on) and your backup options. Also ask what services they provide, what specials they may run, and if they offer any package deals. Record the included services and costs of all options. For example, a flower shop may have a bridal package with a dedicated number of bouquets, centerpieces, and church decorations. It may also charge considerably less for in-season selections or less involved arrangements.

Request any available information and all estimates in writing. Ask about deposit and final payment schedules. Check out their cancellation and refund policies, and secure references or samples.

Once you have nailed down the major points and prices, roll up your sleeves and ask them what other additional charges may apply. Often, even written quotes only provide the costs for specified services. They may not include extra fees for delivery, overtime, and taxes. Are the waiters and their tips included? What about setup and cleanup? Is there a rental charge for place settings and glassware?

What are you are responsible for? Do you need to provide the band with a stage and an electric source for an outdoor event? Can they set it up for an additional fee? Are you expected to provide meals for each of the band members? By taking the time to thoroughly investigate your options in your first meetings, you may save yourself time—and a few surprises—down the road.

40.

Learn to Say No

While compromise plays an integral role in any family function, including your wedding, there will be times that you will need to stick to your guns. The wishes of you and your husband-to-be are the ones that count most. Your desires are what need to be met. If they present a major conflict with someone else's good intentions, it may be time to make a stand.

Your mother may have looked beautiful in grandma's wedding gown, but *you* do not have to wear it. Be sure to tell your mom how much you appreciate her thoughtfulness. Then make it a point to let her know—immediately, so that she does not get the wrong impression—that you already have a style in mind for your own dress. Or perhaps remind her of "your superstition regarding used wedding gowns."

Just because your sister cannot possibly imagine an evening without her four-year-old son does not mean that you need to make an exception to your adults-only reception (regardless of how much your other relatives may pressure you to do so). It is, ultimately, your sister's choice whether to stay at home or hire a baby-sitter.

And you may find that vendors can be extremely persuasive. Be especially vigilant regarding your own intentions when dealing with them. Of course, your caterer will suggest that you serve filet mignon. An entire roomful of exotic flowers *may* be an exquisite alternative to your red-rose-and-baby's-breath centerpieces. And the diamond-studded headpiece might make a nice complement to your gown. Take a few days to consider your options before signing on the dotted line of any extravagant new additions to your original plans.

You are the bride and the hostess. Your decisions deserve to be respected. They will be, if you stand firmly behind them. In some cases, you may find that the best course of action is to just say "No, thank you."

41.

Plan and Protect Your
Beauty Confidence

As women, we tend to put everything—and everyone else— first. Then, if there is a leftover minute or two, we care for ourselves. Remember that your wedding day is called "your day" for a reason. And on your day, don't you want to be your most beautiful you? Be sure to plan and protect your beauty confidence.

Some women gain confidence with a professional makeover and hairstyle. Some prefer a facial and a manicure. And still others want a relaxing yoga class followed by a walk on the beach. Regardless of what your secrets are, make it a point to book firm appointments for *all* of your beauty needs well in advance of your ceremony.

Schedule time for personal primping just as thoroughly as you do the professional appointments. Some women find that a half-hour of meditation clears their heads. Others swear that self-bronzing lotions give them an irresistible glow. Reserving these sessions will assure that you are not like the bride who refused to remove her gloves throughout the entire evening because her nail polish was chipped.

Most of these glamorizing acts will need to be performed during the week before the wedding. That's okay. The week is preserved for the sake of your composure. And what could be more composing than having complete beauty confidence on your day?

42.

Indulge Yourself
in the Menu

There is nothing more crucial to a hearty gala than good food. After all, a fine meal in itself can be worth a celebration. Whether the event calls for a formal sit-down supper or a barbecue buffet lunch, savory morsels will elevate any atmosphere.

It is certainly worth the effort to be a little creative and a little finicky when it comes to choosing the cuisine. In short, personalize the meal to your discriminating taste buds.

You and your sweetheart will want to personally select each part of the meal. Each course should stand out on its own and work equally well with the others. Composing your own menu can be even more fun.

Take a look at the presentation of your meal. Visually appealing foods already taste better than those just plopped onto a plate. If you are planning a banquet, how do you intend to set up the serving table to look good, as well as keep foods at their proper temperatures? Also be sure to choose wines and champagnes that complement both the flavor and the quality of the rest of the meal. Last, but far from least, are the seating arrangements. Are the chairs and tables comfortable?

Whatever foods you choose to serve, do so as part of an overall dining experience. If the cuisine, presentation, and seating all pass your high standards, your guests will walk away with the memory of a great meal—and a great celebration.

43.

Set the Mood with Music

The location, the food served, and the decorations are all frameworks for the tone of a wedding. But nothing sets the mood like music. Be sure that this mood matches the overall style of your reception. You may decide on a reggae band for a beach party, a string quartet for an elegant tea, or a top-forty band at a reception hall. Many couples also opt to hire a deejay to spin the tunes, or ask a friend to oversee prerecorded selections. However you choose to handle the entertainment, there are two considerations to be met—the ceremony and the reception.

Since the ceremony is your union of love, select a musical theme that warms up the room and prepares your audience for the mood that you are creating. A change in tempo will announce the beginning of the ceremony, as well as the arrival of the bride. Use whatever song moves you. This can be anything from the soothing sounds of Sade to the tried and true "Here Comes the Bride" (otherwise known as Wagner's "Bridal Chorus" from *Lohengrin*).

It is just as important for your reception to have music that fits it. Do you envision a gathering of quiet smiles and conversation, or a fast-moving party with everyone dancing? Take a moment to consider your guests' ages and preferences. Then personalize the entertainment to keep both you and your guests in high spirits.

44.

Preserve Your Wedding Memories

C hoosing a wedding photographer used to mean just that — you hired someone to take pictures of your wedding. Simple.

Today's technology, however, has introduced an endless array of ways to preserve your wedding ceremony. All photography studios that cater to brides offer portraits and packages of still shots. Most photographers now also provide VHS video services. Many have ventured into the world of DVDs and live Web transmissions.

After reviewing the choices and often high costs of professional photography, an engaged couple may be tempted to ask a friend or relative, someone they know is an amateur photographer, to take all of their pictures. This is usually not a good idea. Creative friends and family members can be a blessing for getting candid shots. But for these, you can place disposable cameras on each dining table and let guests snap away. Your loved ones can help to fill in the gaps. For instance, a couple who opts to save money by hiring a photographer for the ceremony and early reception hours only may ask a friend to cover the bride's morning preparations and final hours of the celebration. But in general, you will need a professional to truly capture the moments and emotions of your wedding day.

When shopping for a photographer, review a portfolio of recent work. Look for keepsake albums that unfold like a storybook. Make sure that the photographer whose work you review is the one who will be taking the photographs. Compare the packages being offered and get your final decisions guaranteed in writing.

Do the same for a videographer. Watch any demo tapes closely. Both the video and the audio portions should be clear and steady, with smooth transitions between events. Know exactly what is included in the price quote. Elaborately polished videos often include such special effects as background music, titles, and childhood photos. Each of these additions will increase the final cost.

New technology, such as DVD production and editing, streaming online videos, and live Web transmissions, may vary widely in quality and cost. Ensure that the vendor has adequate experience in this technical endeavor.

Once you have chosen your professionals, be sure that they know in advance the sequence of events in your wedding and reception. Tell them which shots are the most important to you and give them a list of your VIP guests. By carefully reviewing and preparing your photographic specialists in advance, you can be confident that the memories of your wedding day will be properly preserved for the future.

45.

Break Away from Bridal Guilt

Planning a wedding can be demanding. At some point, brides may find that they're not spending as much time with their friends. You may have had to give up volunteer work, or forgo sending your usually elaborate birthday gifts. And just when was the last time you walked the dog? You may start to feel guilty that the organizing is taking up too much of your time and spending money.

Then there are the wedding plans themselves. You may find yourself worried about stretching your budget. Or find it hard to talk to the sweet old widow next door, knowing that she is not invited. Or you can't sleep at night because you didn't hire your brother's heavy-metal rock band as the entertainment.

Sometimes, guilt can act as a good force, since it keeps us in check regarding the feelings of others. Most of the time, however, our emotions of guilt are actually fears of rejection. We are afraid that if we let someone down, that if we don't make them happy, we will lose their approval.

We have to let go of the notion that we can please everyone all of the time. As women, especially, we tend to hold ourselves responsible for everyone else's happiness. But this happiness can come with a high price tag. We may sacrifice our own wishes for those of others. And that leads to another type of guilt—better known as resentment.

Remember that this is your day. If ever there is a time to be a little selfish, it's now. Your friends recognize that you have other priorities. Your dog won't need therapy due to neglect. Your bank account will probably recover. And if your brother doesn't get the gig, he won't hate you forever.

Let go of bridal guilt. No one can ever make everyone happy all of the time. Worrying about it takes up far more time and energy than is deserved. There is only one person that you have to please right now—and that is you.

46

Rule the Weight Game

From the moment that you sign the deposit check for your wedding gown, your attention shifts from the yards of delicate fabric to the inches around your waistline. This is true of almost all women, regardless of whether they wear a size 4 or a size 14.

Bridal shop sales assistants quite often encounter future brides who order a dress in a smaller size, in anticipation of a future body in a smaller size. Salespeople report that they unanimously advise against this strategy.

"Brides do frequently lose weight before their day," states one such saleslady. "Which is why the fittings are so important. But we do not recommend ordering a smaller-sized gown since dresses can be taken in easily."

But what if you *gain* a few pounds? It's not uncommon. Stress and anxiety can steal away your appetite or predispose you to nervous eating. Often, planning a wedding has brides so busy that many engaged women find themselves wolfing down chips from the gas station rather than stopping for a healthy meal. They may then feel guilty the next day and nibble on lettuce, only to lose the battle to an ice cream craving later in the night. It can become a vicious cycle.

That doesn't mean that you can't shed a little cushioning before your walk down the aisle. It simply means that you need to stand back and listen to your common sense. You know that cutting back on your portions, skipping desserts, and adding an extra hour to your weekly exercise routine will make you a little leaner. And you also know that starving equals bingeing equals the nasty little side effect of weight gain.

So take it slowly, and be realistic. Otherwise, you may just find yourself begging the seamstress to add expansion panels to your gown at the last minute. That's far from what you envisioned when you first ordered the dress.

47.

Honor Your Body

drenaline is a magical drug. It can keep your body running at full speed when you would have otherwise collapsed long ago. Organizing a wedding is an adrenaline-packed process.

But as we all know, adrenaline is merely a reaction to its counterpart—stress. And both can wear you out pretty quickly. Once your system is out of balance, you can lose your mental edge and also may become quite susceptible to aches and illnesses. At one time or another, each of us has experienced a forced "time-out."

Fortunately, your body will usually tell you when you've pushed it too far, before you are *forced* to slow down. Your job is to simply listen and respect your own needs.

Sleep is one requirement that we tend to forgo when our lives are hectic. If you find yourself yawning at the office or asking people to repeat themselves because you aren't listening, then it's time to take a night off—just to sleep. Reschedule any obligations that you may have. Pick up supper on the way home. Set out what you need (including your outfit) for the morning. Then drift into an early slumber, knowing that tomorrow is taken care of. Take as many "sleep nights" as your body requires.

Nutrition is another way that we cheat ourselves when other priorities get in the way. Again, listen to your body. What foods make you feel good? Salads? Fresh fish? Whole grains? Dried fruits? Stock up on these nourishing items at home, and work to avoid self-destructing potato chip marathons.

It's easy to skip a workout to schedule a fitting—but what happens when you find yourself snapping at everyone in your way? You need some stress release. Your body knows when a good stretch, a brisk walk, or your favorite dance class is in order. By honoring your body leading up to your wedding, you can be reasonably certain that your body will remain strong on the day that you need it the most.

48.

Don't Listen to the
"What Ifs"

There are certain backup plans that are vital, such as cover for an outdoor wedding in the event of inclement weather. And then there are things that you have absolutely no control over. Yes, it is possible that the church will burn down the night before the ceremony. Conceivably, a tornado could strike town. And your fiancé might just faint before he can spit out the words, "I do."

Accept that there are things beyond your control. Also accept that worrying about them will not change the outcome. Things are bound to go wrong. All the little mistakes that can pile up are just that—small, unimportant gaffes that no one but you (and your mother) will notice. If the flowers are missing a particular blossom from the bouquet, or the bridesmaids walk down the aisle in the wrong order, take a deep breath and laugh. When the band plays the wrong song for you and your groom, ask for another dance and enjoy the extra time in the spotlight. Years from now, you will look back on any mishaps with amusement. Remembering what is important now will make your wedding more meaningful and allow you to focus on the big picture.

Worrying about the things that are out of your control will merely waste precious energy that you may need elsewhere. You, your fiancé, family, and friends are what make a wedding special. Everything else is just icing on the cake!

49.

He May Not Be
Detail-Oriented

Face the facts: Many men are not detail-oriented. It may sound sexist, but in general, men rely on us to organize their households, their appointments, and their offices. Often, women are simply better at this small stuff.

The same holds true for your wedding. Do not be alarmed when the bright-eyed enthusiasm that he displayed while you were choosing invitations wanes by the time you're writing out seating charts.

It's not that he's not interested. He may simply not comprehend all of those little details. And he doesn't quite understand how you keep track of it all, either, on top of your job responsibilities and other duties that you handle.

Your fiancé may respond to the pressure in a variety of ways. Some men face it directly by telling their brides-to-be that the intricate planning is in her capable hands. Other men suddenly acquire a passion for a seasonal sport that claims their attention during the pre-wedding activities. Still others find this a great time to throw themselves into an important business project.

However, most grooms-to-be just tune the subject out when things get too involved. Often, all that they really want to know is when and where to show up. The rest is up to you.

Try not to get upset and accuse him of not caring about the details. His primary concern is simply that you are happy. That's not such a bad thing. *His* fantasy wedding may be an exchange of vows between the sixth and seventh green, celebrated with a beer.

So keep him informed of the major developments. Let him know if there is a glitch. Ask his opinion when it's important. But respect that your fiancé may not be detail-oriented about this particular event. Don't overload him with information. It may just scare him away from the entire planning process.

Do, however, be sure that he knows when and where to show up. Otherwise, you may need to chase him down at the eighth green.

50.

Recognize the
Most Valuable Wedding Gifts

Most of your friends and relatives would love to avoid the department store and give you a personal wedding gift, if only they knew what you wanted. You may find that you can add special touches to your plans—or even save money on budgeted items—if you request certain wedding gifts from certain people.

Why not ask your cousin—who happens to be a licensed masseuse—for a couple's massage the week before the wedding? Not only is that the time that the both of you will really need some relaxation, but it is certainly better then unwrapping yet another toaster oven.

Do you have a friend with a mountain cabin or a seaside cottage? Borrowing their digs for a week might be the perfect honeymoon retreat. Is your girlfriend an interior designer? How valuable will her services be when you and your betrothed attempt to reconcile your decorating styles into one home?

There are a couple of guidelines to keep in mind when requesting personalized wedding gifts, however. First, be sure that the person whom you are asking knows that this favor is considered to be his wedding gift to you. Write a thank you card for his services at the same time that you send out the rest of your wedding gift appreciation notes.

Do not ask anyone for a service that will detract from that person's enjoyment as a guest at your ceremony or reception. For example, you may request that your amateur photographer uncle take some candid shots during the later part of the festivities. But asking him to photograph the event from beginning to end makes him a paid professional rather than a guest.

Remember that professionalism counts. Having Aunt Beth bake a few dozen of her famous sugar cookies in lieu of the caterer providing dessert can save you money and allow your aunt to give you a gift that you both treasure. However, suggesting that your sister, who is a "pretty good cook," cater the main dish of the affair could spell disaster.

Lastly, carefully evaluate the wedding services that are offered to you as gifts. Just because your girlfriend can carve out a clown cake for her four-year-old might not mean that she is the best candidate to create your wedding cake. And although it is awfully nice of your nephew to offer the free services of his band for your reception entertainment, some gifts are better off left in the package.

51.

Release Doubt

At one time or another, nearly every bride experiences the wedding blues. In the face of a major, life-changing commitment, she may start to have her doubts. "Is he really the one?" or "Am I ready for this?" she might wonder. And she should. Marriage is one of the biggest decisions in your life. In one way or another, it will most likely affect you forever.

The most productive way to handle these perfectly normal fears is to explore them. Is it your fiancé that's making you nervous? Is it the act of marriage? Or is this just a case of stage fright while thinking about the upcoming ceremony?

When doubt strikes, take a few minutes of quiet time to work through it. While nothing is for certain, close your eyes and picture yourself growing old with your groom. Is the image clear or hazy? If it is hazy, why? Are there certain aspects of your beloved that concern you?

Obviously, no one is perfect. Not him. Not you. Can you live with his flaws? Do you think he can live with yours? Are you truly in love?

Perhaps your worries lie within yourself. Marriage is a monumental step. Are you ready? As humans, we tend to fear change. Again, it's perfectly normal. You may simply be nervous about upcoming life changes. Or does it run deeper than that?

You may also be experiencing pre-wedding jitters. You've spent months planning this day. Soon, you will be the center of attention for all that goes right and all that goes wrong.

Ask yourself if you would be this anxious if you were getting married at a drive-through chapel in Las Vegas. If that doesn't relieve your panic, spend a night reviewing your wedding agenda. Take control of your planning, rather than allowing it to control you.

Only you can make the final decisions regarding your mate and your marriage. But everyone has doubts. The best way to handle them is to recognize them and explore them. Either act on them — or release them. Then turn your energies elsewhere.

52.

Speak Up When
It Becomes Too Much

There will be some days that you actually find yourself adding more things onto your wedding to-do list than you are crossing off. These will also be the days that you dream about canceling the whole event and eloping to a third-world country.

Before booking your plane ticket, try these magic words: "Mom, do you mind stopping by the bridal shop to make sure that my dress came in as ordered?" "Dad, could you please make the hotel reservations for your brother?" "Sweetheart, I need a night out to relax and forget about all of this."

As women, we often don't even consider asking for help. Aren't we, after all, the ones who are used to helping everybody else?

When it starts to become too much, take a close look at your list. What can you ask someone else to do today or tomorrow? How can you create a little down time for yourself without loading up next week's responsibilities, which will only create more stress?

Isolate areas where you could use an extra set of hands. Then speak up. Ask for the help you need *before* you are tempted to call the whole thing off. Most airline tickets are, after all, nonrefundable purchases.

53.

Express Your Feelings

You may be nervous. You are probably tired. There seem to be new decisions to make every day. The pressure can sometimes build up—and take your blood pressure right along with it. You may find yourself wanting to snap at everyone around you.

At times like this, it is probably best to hold your tongue. So you heard through the grapevine that your mother-in-law does not agree with your musical selection. Is it really worth the energy to argue with her? Not everyone is going to agree with your choices. The final decisions are yours, so don't waste time defending them.

There will be times, however, when is it important to express your feelings. This is especially true when the issue could become problematic down the line. For instance, if you are wondering why your maid of honor has not arranged for the bridal shower, ask her. It may be that she is thrilled to throw you a party; she simply did not realize that it was one of her duties.

Perhaps your father has not gotten back to you about the travel arrangements that he agreed to make. Or your mother expects you to wear her wedding gown, but you want to choose your own. If a heart-to-heart conversation is in order, then have one. You may well avoid a heated eruption later.

By the same token, make it a point to also express your positive feelings. Pick up the phone to call someone who has gone out of his or her way to help you. Or better yet, send a small thank you card. Mailing a single line of prose — "I don't know what I'd do without you" — can lift both of your spirits.

During the wedding planning process, every bride's emotions are running high. The trick is to let go of the small details that are not worth getting upset over, and gently confront the things that do matter before they become problems that may cause you anxiety.

54.

Let Go of the Details

By allowing yourself to request and accept help from your friends, you must also learn to let go of the details. Many brides feel that this is their day, and they want everything to be absolutely perfect. Yet chances are that every detail will not be perfect—no matter how much you may worry about them. In the end, most of those pesky little specifics really do not matter anyway.

We all know people who get so focused on the incidentals that they lose sight of the whole, and we have probably all been guilty of that at one time or another. Be aware that as a bride, it may be easy to fall into that trap. Why direct your energies toward the lesser issues when you have larger priorities on your list?

Okay, so your friends weaved the centerpieces with baby blue ribbon instead of sky blue, like you wanted. Your mother ordered the smaller version of the jewelry boxes that you plan to give as bridesmaid's gifts. The caterer just informed you that asparagus is out of season, so you'll have to serve cream of broccoli soup instead.

There are so many small details which make up a wedding—it helps to remember that any one or two going awry is not going to have a noticeable effect on your day. As a matter of fact, if you can avoid even knowing about these changes, all the better. What you don't know can't hurt you, or at the very least, stress you out. Encourage those closest to you and the planning to take charge and make executive decisions. By the time that your day comes around, you will be grateful that other people are willing to take charge!

Before allowing the trivial things to upset you, ask yourself if any of this will really matter five years from now. Then be grateful to your friends, your parents, and your caterer for their help.

55.

Distinguish Good Advice
from Bad Advice

So...you're getting married...." You can expect to hear this expression several times in the upcoming months. And it usually precedes the speaker's intention to share with you some free advice.

We all know what free advice is worth. So before you allow yourself to be persuaded in any way by someone else's wisdom, you need to consider two things—the advice itself, and the source.

Some hints from friends may be quite valuable. After all, each of us has accumulated some useful knowledge during our many years here on earth. But that doesn't mean that every technique will work for every couple.

One of the most common pieces of advice you will hear is, "Never go to bed angry." There are husbands and wives who swear by this philosophy. But there are just as many people who find that a night of sleep clears their heads. In the morning, they wonder why they were so angry, and realize that they may have overreacted to a situation. For these couples, a night of sleep can actually solve many of their differences.

Whether or not the advice *sounds* valid, remember to consider the source. Who are you going to believe? Your thrice-divorced aunt, who is pushing you to write up a prenuptial agreement, or your best friend, who has been blissfully married for twenty years and advocates trust instead of legal bindings?

Humorously, your commitment-phobic friends always seem to be the first to offer up some advice. It is almost a guarantee that at least one established bachelor or bachelorette will tell you: "Congratulations. Don't do it."

There are also people who have their own best interests at heart. Your girlfriends may be jealous of your relationship if they suspect that you will no longer be spending as much time with them. And can you really believe anything that coworker who has a crush on you says?

In the long run, you may hear a gem or two of advice. But in the meantime, you will most likely need to sift through a lot of nonsense to find those gems. So listen to the well-intended words, and then measure their validity by listening to your own heart.

56.

Let Go of
Other People's Conflicts

"**H**is two aunts have not spoken in years. "How *could* you invite *her* to the wedding?" they each cry. Your brother has refused to eat at the restaurant where your rehearsal dinner will be held ever since the night that he found a hair in his food. He plans to skip the rehearsal completely in protest. And your maid of honor is complaining to everyone who will listen about your choice in bridesmaids' gowns. After all, she *told* you that reds make her complexion look ruddy. Some friend you are!

Almost every bride will hear discontent regarding some aspect of her guest list or arrangements. In many instances, the issues are isolated. Some may even border on trivial. Before you allow other people's issues to steer you off course, evaluate the validity of the grievance.

It is quite understandable if your conservative parents are not comfortable attending a beach ceremony at a nudist resort, and a compromise may need to be made. However, if they have announced that they will boycott your (fully clothed) outdoor wedding because they prefer an indoor religious ceremony, they may simply be attempting to strong-arm you into changing your plans.

Do not allow yourself to be blackmailed into shaping your day around someone else's desires. And do not let other people foist their own issues onto your shoulders. Recognize that others need to deal with their own conflicts, no matter how much they may complain (unfairly) to you. Your plate is full. Scratch "Make everybody happy" off of your to-do list. Then let their conflicts go.

57.

Ask for
What You Want

Wedding gifts are as traditional as weddings themselves. Most gifts, from a straw hut to a live pig to a few clay pots, were designed to help the new couple begin their life together.

Although the nature of the gifts themselves may have changed, the spirit in which they are given has not. In other words, wedding gifts are still a way for the members of the community to celebrate and support the new union within their circle.

Yet many brides feel a twinge of guilt when they write out a gift list or create a bridal registry. Second-time brides, especially, may even be tempted to spread the word that they do not want presents. Not only are these ladies cheating themselves, they are also depriving others of the opportunity to share in their joy by helping them to establish their new households.

Creating a gift list or a registry is not a selfish act. On the contrary, as long as the requests are reasonable and include items in all price ranges, they actually do your guests a favor. They allow your friends and family to purchase meaningful things while avoiding countless hours of shopping and several phone calls so as not to duplicate other people's gifts.

If you choose to write up a gift list, distribute it in halves or thirds to your mother, mother-in-law, or talkative friend. Then step back. Your work is done. If someone does ask you what you want for your wedding, ask that person to call one of your gift-list keepers.

Creating a registry can take a little more time, but it can also be a lot of fun. Think of it as going on a shopping spree without spending any money. Today's bride can register her wishes in a variety of places and ways. Discount stores, department stores, hardware stores, plant nurseries, travel boutiques, bookshops, and even office supply warehouses now offer bridal registries. Many of the choices can be made in person, online, or by catalogue.

Don't feel obligated to register at only one place, but do keep your out-of-town guests in mind. Give them the option of a national (or at least regional) chain or an online venue to do their shopping. And by the way, no matter how many people may ask you where you registered, the only appropriate place to actually write the information is on the shower invitation. By steering your guests in the right direction, you will be helping them to purchase the gifts that you want and need.

58.

Remember Personal Priorities
in Your Budget

There will be many last-minute items on your bridal to-do list that can add up in cost quite quickly. When detailing your budget, don't forget to include your personal needs.

Even if you happen to be fortunate enough to have parents who are able and willing to pick up the majority of your wedding expenses, you and your soon-to-be husband will need to contribute a certain amount of out-of-pocket funds. One of the first expenses that you should address with these funds is yourself.

Chances are that you will soon wish to purchase a honeymoon wardrobe, extra salon visits, and your bridal lingerie. Some women include facials, massages, or tanning booth visits to their list of prenuptial needs.

Take a moment to consider what items will give you the most peace of mind during the height of your wedding planning. Perhaps a few nights of restaurant meals will give you extra time to organize.

Or you may feel more confident about being center stage if you hire a professional makeup artist to prepare you for your bridal debut. Would extra honeymoon spending cash allow you to enjoy the trip without worry?

Be sure to take your personal needs into account when you create your budget. Then treat them with the same priority that you do any other necessary expense.

59.

Succeed at
Long-Distance Planning

Organizing a wedding over distance is a brave, but not impossible, task. In some cases, a couple may decide that it is simply more guest-friendly to hold their ceremony in another city or state, such as their hometown. Other wedding partners choose to exchange nuptials in an exotic location many miles away.

Whatever the circumstances may be, any bride is certain to encounter different sets of concerns if she is holding her ceremony in a faraway place. Those issues can easily be alleviated with a little additional organization.

Remember your time frame. Chances are that you will be making at least one (and in many cases only one) visit to your wedding location prior to the event. Your time will be limited. Make the most of your trip by spending a few hours on the telephone before you head out. Get as many details, quotes, and menus as you can beforehand, so that your days there are well spent with appointments and decision-making. While you are in your wedding town, don't forget your personal needs. Try out and schedule a hairdresser, manicurist, and makeup professional for the event.

Delegate, delegate, delegate. Anyone who lives in the area or knows the location well can be helpful. Ask your local friends and family to do some legwork so that your time in town is productive. They can check out banquet halls, restaurants, florists, bands, and caterers to narrow down your list of potential vendors.

Find storage and transportation for your things. You will be traveling back and forth with many items such as bridalwear, gifts, luggage for your honeymoon, and anything special that you may decide to bring along for the wedding. Unless you plan to drive straight to the wedding in a pickup truck and drive straight home, it may help to enlist friends and family to help keep and move your things. The more items that you can stash in someone's closet at the site of your ceremony, the less you will be worried about on the days before your wedding. Can you enlist friends or a package service to help transport some of your necessities to their final destination? Can you get your wedding gifts back home utilizing the same friends or package service—especially if you and your betrothed are headed straight to your honeymoon?

Take care of money issues. What if local vendors do not accept out-of-state checks? Does your bank have a branch in the city where you will be wed? It may be advantageous to secure bank checks or completed money orders prior to your trip. If differing currency is a concern, check with your local bank about exchange rates and traveler's checks. Be aware that not all countries accept all credit cards. Relying on a particular credit card may leave you scrambling to find last-minute funds. What about getting all of those cash gifts home? Perhaps a trusted family member can deposit the funds and send you a single check. Or you can wire the funds home through a local bank for a minimal fee. Either way is better than toting several checks or large amounts of cash around through airports and truck stops.

Allow yourself to rest. While it may be necessary to schedule your grooming appointments the day before your ceremony, give yourself the prior day off. Travel is tiring. Wedding preparations can be exhausting. And what groom wants to lift his bride's veil to find dark circles under her eyes? A full day—or at least one relaxed evening—to catch up your energy should be an essential part of your travel agenda.

Take the time to iron out the special concerns of long-distance organization in advance. It can go a long way toward ensuring a wrinkle-free event in a faraway place.

60.

Embrace Visiting Guests
from a Distance

One of the most endearing aspects of any wedding is the opportunity to catch up with rarely seen friends and family. An engaged couple, however, may find themselves torn between the desire to take care of their out-of-town guests and the time needed to fulfill their own obligations.

It is helpful to plan for your visitors early on, provide them with any information that they may need, and then leave them to their own devices during their stay. Keep in mind that you and your mate will not have the time to send out maps, pick people up from the airport, or make hotel reservations. In general, guests should be responsible for their own arrangements, including transportation to the wedding. It is customary—though by no means expected—for the bride's and groom's families to find or finance accommodations for their own immediate relatives.

Stop and take a deep breath before you offer your own home to any bunking visitors. Entertaining company will be the last thing on your mind on the big day. On the other hand, having your maid of honor stay with you could be a wonderful bonding experience, and she can provide you with all sorts of last-minute help.

Appoint a travel agent with a toll-free phone number to find a group rate at a local hotel with airport shuttle service. A hotel that you already plan to use for the rehearsal dinner or reception may be the most obliging place to start. The advantage of using agents is that they may also assist your loved ones with flight or rental car reservations. Remember that travel agents are free of charge to you or your guests since they collect their fees from the airlines and hotels.

Have the agent (or a helpful friend) arrange for the hotel concierge to place brochures of local attractions, restaurants, transportation services, and maps in each guest's room. This package can include a short "welcome letter" from you, along with any additional information that your guests may need.

Finally, make sure that your parents and your parents-in-law both have the contact numbers of the travel agent and designated hotel. As you receive RSVP cards from traveling guests, ask your family to pass along the information. Your visitors may choose to stay elsewhere. That's okay. You have offered to "take care of them" while balancing the time needed for your other obligations.

61.

Give from Your Heart
to the Wedding Party

With everything that needs to be done and all of the expenses mounting up, is it really necessary to buy gifts for members of the wedding party? By their very nature, gifts are never mandatory. They are a sentiment from the heart, and are not to be expected by the giver or the receiver.

However, bridesmaid's and groomsmen's gifts are considered to be good etiquette. Moreover, you may find yourself relying heavily on your friends to help with your wedding preparations. Tokens of recognition will not only comfort your mind, they will also serve to remind your friends that their efforts are appreciated.

Gifts can be something simple that the receiver can wear during the ceremony, such as pendants for the ladies and cuff links for the men. Or they may be for future enjoyment. A special bottle of wine, engraved jewelry boxes, or theater tickets (two for each attendant) will leave your friends with the promise of memories to come.

Additionally, a number of other people may also deserve to be recognized in a special way; for example, the sister who bakes all of the cookies for the reception or the cousin who shuttles guests back and forth to the airport.

Don't forget about your groom. Why not give him a romantic reminder of the most important occasion of your lives together? Many couples exchange a special piece of jewelry or another intimate gift on their wedding day.

The gifts that you give to your wedding attendants should be special. Take a few moments early in your planning stages to choose something that lets your friends know the value of their participation and assistance to you.

62.

Consider Skipping
the Attendants' Parties

Traditional American weddings have never been a single event, but rather a series of events. These nuptial-related festivities may include (among others):

- An engagement party (hosted by the bride's family)
- A bridal luncheon (given for the bride by her attendants)
- A bridesmaids' luncheon for the bridal party and a bachelor dinner for the groomsmen, or a single attendants' party for both
- A bridal shower (hosted by the bride's friends)
- A bachelor party (hosted by the groom's friends)
- A groom's mother's luncheon (given by, obviously, the groom's mother)
- A rehearsal dinner, following the wedding rehearsal
- A wedding breakfast (hosted by the bride's family to entertain out-of-town guests on the morning of the event)

After so much socializing, it is nearly amazing that anyone has the energy left to actually get married. Today, many couples choose to combine or pass up on a number of these customary celebrations. In fact, due to distance and economics, it may be preferable to keep the parties to a minimum.

Whichever events you, your spouse, and your families choose to coordinate is up to you. The two most important celebrations are your wedding (of course) and the rehearsal dinner. Today, the rehearsal dinner typically serves double duty as an attendants' party, where bridesmaids' and groomsmen's gifts are exchanged.

Start with those two events as your base, and add on however many other celebrations that you believe will be necessary. Just be sure to leave yourself enough energy to say "I do" without yawning.

63.

Include Your Children
in the Celebration

Hundreds of years ago, the primary purpose of a marriage was procreation: to increase the tribe, further the race, and ensure future survival. Today, we still embrace elements of that philosophy, but in a wider spectrum. Modern marriage is about creating a family. That may mean joining individuals into a core family of two. Or it may signify the union of two separate families into one. Brides, grooms, or both may already have their own children. And those children are an integral part of your new relationship. Therefore, it is common these days for children of the engaged couple to be included in the ceremony. Not only does this remind the child of her value, it also reinforces the family commitment. This is especially important for young children who may not be completely comfortable with idea of a new "mommy" or "daddy."

There are many ways to include your children in the ceremony. They can carry out the traditional duties of ring-bearer or flower girl, or their roles may be improvised. A young daughter may accompany her mother on her walk down the aisle, while a son waits beside the groom for the bride to arrive. Pairs of children of any age may have their own places in the procession, ahead of or behind the bridesmaids. Older sons may give the bride away. Daughters may serve as bridesmaids. Either may provide a special role, such as reciting a poem or reading a significant piece.

Even if your wedding is an adults-only event, it is quite understandable to include your own children. However, it may not be a bad idea to arrange a sitter for the reception. It is never a bad idea to let your children — and children-to-be — know just how valuable they are to you and your new family union.

64.

Negotiate with
the Underwriter

The financiers of your wedding, who are typically you, your fiancé, and/or your parents and his parents, all deserve special attention. Your families, certainly, warrant special gratitude and respect. Since they are under no obligation to absorb your wedding costs, whatever they do contribute is a gift. Unfortunately, this is why some problems may occur. Some gifts may come with strings attached.

Oftentimes, those who help to sponsor the function may feel as though they have a certain amount of control over the decisions. And, in essence, they do. More than one bride has changed her plans to comply with the wishes of someone else—the "someone else" being the person who threatened to cut off her financing.

One way to circumvent potential problems, of course, is for the couple to pay for the entire affair themselves. Another way is to treat the opinions of your parents with respect. This does not mean that you need to abandon your own dreams for theirs. It simply means that a little communication and understanding can go a long way toward a great compromise.

Perhaps a bride's parents have offered to pay for her ceremony and reception. Her parents have a vision of the event in mind which is altogether different from what the bride and groom want! What are the true issues? Are religious beliefs or business obligations coloring the situation? Do the bride's beliefs clash with those of her benefactors? Each person's needs deserve respect, at the very least.

Although the final wedding decisions will be made by you and your mate, a little understanding and respect, and perhaps some compromise, are in order. They may help to keep relations with your contributors on a friendly note.

65.

Create a Paperwork Date Night

C ar insurance policies, bank records, social security data—it all needs to be changed. Who knew that getting married could require so much paperwork? Rather than face the growing pile of forms and documents with dread, why not turn all of that busywork into an enjoyable evening project?

Give yourselves enough lead time to collect as many change forms as you can. Women who plan to take their spouse's name will obviously have more records to change than ones who keep their original names, as will any partner who intends to relocate after the ceremony.

There may be some revisions that require a copy of your marriage certificate. Even though you will not have the documentation in hand until a future date, why not complete and stamp these forms while you are tackling the pile? Later, you can simply make multiple photocopies of your legal license to send off with this (otherwise finalized) paperwork.

Plan a date with your beloved. Reserve some quiet time. Place an order for food. Then make a game of the pencil-pushing. Try completing each other's forms to see how much you really know about the other person. For example, what's his social security number? His birth year? His mother's maiden name?

If you are also filling out change of address forms, how well do you know each other's address books? Ask him about his friends. Share stories with him about how you met some of your friends. Learn the names of your groom's distant relatives' spouses and children.

Aside from personal contacts, the following is a partial list of the records that you may need to alter:

- Social security records
- Automobile and other vehicle insurance policies
- Life insurance policies
- Health insurance policies
- Homeowner's and liability insurance policies
- Driver's licenses
- Credit card accounts
- Voter registration records
- Leases
- Immigration records
- Investment accounts and records
- Employment records

Good luck with your paperwork!

66.

Let Your Friends
Shower You with Attention

"I'm not sure if I want a bridal shower," more than one humble bride-to-be has stated. "Isn't it just a way to get gifts?" Yes, it is. But before shying away from a shower, consider this: The occasion is not about *getting* gifts. It's about *giving* gifts.

The wedding ceremony originated as a community event. It was cause for celebration for an entire village when two young people came together to unite. The townswomen celebrated by preparing the bride for her upcoming role as wife. They "showered" their younger sister with advice, food staples, and household objects to help equip her for her new duties.

Today, much of the advice-giving has been replaced by game-playing. And not many brides receive food staples—such as flour and salt—wrapped up in pretty paper. However, the essential philosophy of the bridal shower has not changed. Your girlfriends still want to help you to prepare for your new life. You can let them in a variety of ways.

Some women prefer the old-fashioned, girls-only party. These affairs provide a wonderful opportunity for fun and laughter. Others may opt for a more modern twist to the traditional affair. For instance, theme showers are becoming popular. These run the gamut from recipe showers to gardening showers to household hardware showers. Another recent trend is toward couples' showers. Coed gatherings can be just as much fun as their counterparts, while shielding the bride-to-be from the embarrassing childhood anecdotes and sparing the guests from assorted games and traditions.

Regardless of which format makes you comfortable, don't eschew the bridal shower out of shyness. The gifts you'll receive are simply a by-product of the shower's true intention, which is for your friends to give you gifts—to help prepare you for your new life.

67.

Acknowledge the Bachelor Party with Grace

Few wedding rituals provoke more arguments between a couple-to-be than the bachelor party. While women are running around organizing flowers, photographers, and seating arrangements, men somehow get rewarded with a night on the town all of their own. And that night often includes—well, who knows what? Let's face it, boys will be boys. They love to be mischievous. There may be an element or two in their evening of fun that you are better off not knowing about.

There are two ways that you can handle the bachelor party: You can react with suspicion, or you can respond with grace.

In the first scenario, you may feel threatened by your fiancé's festivities. You may see it as his way of rebelling against the upcoming wedding. Your imagination tells you that he will be out flirting with beautiful young women to test his desire for you—or even to have one last fling. You may actually convince yourself that the party is a sign that he isn't ready for marriage, and those feelings can cause growing tension in the days leading up to the wedding.

Responding with grace takes trust and self-confidence. As a graceful bride, recognize that the bachelor night is a rite of passage; a male ceremony to mark an *end* to his single days. It also serves as an important reassurance to his buddies that he will remain a friend, even though his priorities will soon be shifting toward family life.

No one is suggesting that you should not feel compelled to make certain, reasonable requests of your beloved. Asking him to appoint a designated driver if there is alcohol involved, for example, is simply a sign that you care for him. On the other hand, making him call you with a report every hour of the night signifies that you do not trust him.

If you do start to feel a little nervous about the bachelor party, try to relax and remember the true reason for the event: Your man is celebrating *because* he is devoting the rest of his life to you. He has found a soul mate, a woman that he wants to be with forever. And *that*, certainly, deserves a toast from his friends.

Show him trust on his big night out. It will remind him how lucky he is to be marrying such a mature person.

68.

Enjoy a Bachelorette Party

These days, not only has the bachelor party become an established tradition for the men involved in a wedding celebration, but a bachelorette party for the women has also increased in popularity. Regardless of whether the evening is directed toward the boys or the girls, the same philosophy of the get-together remains: It is a special time to reinforce your relationships with your same-sex friends. After all, your girlfriends realize that your priorities will soon be shifting toward home and family. Many of them may be terrified that you will transform into Martha Stewart overnight and no longer be interested in their lives, their boyfriends, and their career dilemmas.

The bachelorette party is a valuable reminder to your friends that you still love them; that you will still be on the other end of the phone for them; and that you most certainly *do* want to hear about their work problems. Take an evening to reinforce those bonds with your friends—and let them have their fun with you.

If you really can't stomach a night of cocktails or giddiness, then tailor your last single blowout to better suit your tastes. Why not host a lingerie party? Gather your friends for a day at a photo studio? Spend a few hours gossiping over coffee and cheesecake? Go to a concert? Or plan an old-fashioned slumber party, complete with manicures, pizza, and a pile of chick-flick videos? In the end, it doesn't really matter *how* you spend time with your girlfriends, as long as you spend some time just with your friends.

69.

Pack for Freedom on Your Honeymoon

Your wedding getaway may be a romantic weekend in a nearby mountain cottage, or it may be a two-month-long cruise in the Pacific. Either way, do not be surprised if you and your husband suddenly acquire an insatiable energy for adventure.

After all, your work is done. You are finally married to the person that you love. It's natural to want to let go—to explore the world, and each other.

While packing for your honeymoon, of course bring the clothes that scream "romance" for you and your spouse. But also search your closet for your most comfortable clothes that match the climate of your destination. Remembering how versatile layers can be, collect a few lightweight tops or dresses with matching sweaters that can be wrapped around your neck or waist. Pack the boots, shoes, or sandals that are your most comfortable.

What do you need to carry along to keep yourself looking and feeling your best on a full day's adventure? While this varies from person to person, a glance inside of your purse is a good starting place. Think prepared. Think mobile.

Collect your minimum beauty essentials. Gather any prescription and over-the-counter medications that you use frequently, such as antacids or allergy medicines. Place a day's supply of each into a plastic bag, along with a couple of bandages for potential blisters. Pick up trial sizes of products that you may need specifically for your destination (sunscreen, lip balm, insect repellent). Add to this pile a pen, breath mints, a hair clip, and tissues or wet naps.

Place these in the smallest purse or bag that you can find to accommodate them, that still leaves room for a pair of sunglasses or gloves, a pocket or disposable camera, and a language reference guide (if needed). Be sure the bag has a long enough strap to string around your neck and shoulder for both comfort and safety.

Before journeying out of your suite each morning, replenish your supply of essential items. Tuck in a couple dollars of local currency, one form of identification, a minimum supply of cash or traveler's checks, and only one credit card, along with the phone number of your hotel or tour operator.

Some of your day outings may also require a larger bag, such as a beach bag or a backpack. But for those crazy days that start with breakfast and could end up practically anywhere, you have all of your comfortable essentials at your fingertips. And that gives you freedom to say, "Let's go."

70.

Share Your Joy

There are few things in life that are more joyous than falling in love and embarking on a new life with your chosen mate. Why not share this joy with your close friends and family members?

To one degree, you are already planning to include your loved ones by involving them in and inviting them to your wedding ceremony. So why not take that sentiment a step farther? Why not include your close friends and family members in the excitement of the planning process?

After all, these are the same people that you tend to lean on when you are down. You do not hesitate to pick up the phone for consolation during those times that you are tearful over a fight with your mate; a reprimand by the boss; or a fender-bender on the highway. Isn't it only fair to share your joy in the same way that you often share your misery?

Review your to-do list for the fun tasks. What are the activities that others would enjoy being included in? Taking your grandmother with you when you shop for your wedding dress, for example, will give you both a sentimental memory for years to come. Inviting your in-laws to join you when you sample the caterer's fare is a fun night out for everyone. Wouldn't your friends just love to go to a local club to listen to the band you're considering for your reception? And why not ask you mother to help you choose items for your bridal registry?

By sharing the more exciting aspects of your wedding planning with your friends and family, you can strengthen your bonds with these people and gain invaluable advice on the subject at hand. But most importantly, you are also putting things into balance. Sharing your joy is a thank you gift to your friends—just for being your friends.

71.

Don't Trade Away Your Future

It is likely that before all is said and done, you and your groom will be spending anywhere from a few dollars to tens of thousands of dollars from your own wallets on your wedding. But before committing your credit card limit to your wedding budget, carefully consider where this money is coming from and what impact it may have on your future.

You certainly want your wedding to be special. But remember that your wedding day is only a ritual to symbolize your new life together. Once the ceremony is over, you still have to start that life. And setting up house can be expensive.

Before filling out new credit card applications, applying for a wedding loan, or withdrawing the funds from your 401(k) plan, ask yourself if this debt—or lack of financial security—is a price worth one day in white.

Yes, most couples do receive cash gifts. And in surveys, nearly eighty percent of couples relied upon these funds for their upcoming honeymoon or leftover wedding expenses. Yet many of those same couples responded that they were surprised at how quickly this money was depleted and how little they had left in the end.

Instead of relying upon these finances for your wedding expenses, why not use them for their intended purpose—a financial cushion for your future?

Try to strike a balance between today's wants and tomorrow's needs by determining what funds you have to work with, and then staying within your budget. Avoid letting those little extras chew up your discretionary funds. Just keep in mind that while an outrageously fabulous, fairy-tale wedding may fulfill one dream, you will have other dreams tomorrow. Soon, you may be fantasizing about buying a new home or having a baby. Wouldn't it be nice to be prepared for these upcoming fantasies?

72.

You Can't Make
Everybody Happy

Her family wants them to get married in a Catholic church in Pittsburgh. His family expects that they will recite their nuptials at a synagogue in Florida. Neither set of parents understands "this ridiculous vegetarian craze that the kids are into these days."

So how does the engaged couple keep everybody happy? Quite frankly, they don't. That doesn't mean that there are no compromises to be made. And it certainly does not imply that your friends' and families' wishes should be dismissed without consideration. It is possible to be thoughtful about your loved ones' special needs and requests while still satisfying your own desires. It may, however, require creative thinking.

It is impossible to make everyone happy all of the time, even though women often strive to do so. Additionally, the more that you give in to other people's wishes in the beginning, the more that they may expect you to yield to them throughout the planning process.

When loved ones tell you that they are unhappy with your plans, remember that this is (most likely) not the last time you will encounter this situation. Evaluate their concern. Listen to their input. Determine the true cause of their discontent. Consider your options. Then make the decision that is best for you and your husband-to-be. And let go of *their* disappointment in *your* choices.

73.

Have the Courage
to Call It Off

You've had some doubts. Every man and woman who has ever said "I do" has some reservations. But this is different. There's a gnawing in the pit of your stomach that won't let go. It's not right, and *you know it*. If you have thoroughly explored your fears— and have still come to the conclusion that this is not simply a case of cold feet, that this marriage is truly wrong—then you may just need to take a deep breath and call it off.

Take heart. Many, many people have postponed or cancelled their wedding plans for more reasons than any one of us can imagine. It is a brave step, and one that many people, after the stress and anxiety wear off, are relieved to have taken.

Many new brides and grooms get caught up in the idea of planning a beautiful wedding and looking forward to their future together without checking on the present. When they do finally take stock of the relationship, the thought of breaking someone's heart or angering and disappointing family and friends becomes mortifying. It helps to have more confidence in your loved ones. After all, they only want what is best for you, and will in all likelihood firmly support your decision.

Monetary losses and the inconvenience of returning gifts or changing travel plans is nothing compared to the anger and unhappiness that a future divorce could bring. Most people will admire your courage and stand by you in your time of need.

Canceling a wedding is an enormous decision. There will be consequences—both financial and emotional. Obviously, the earlier you deal with the cancellation, the fewer problems you will encounter.

If—and this is a big "if"—you know in your heart that the marriage is a mistake, then by all means, stop. The mistake of planning a wedding that doesn't happen is miniscule when compared to mistake of saying "I do" when you know that you don't.

74.

Should You Include
Other Children in the Ceremony?

Who can deny the charm of a three-year-old flower girl or a five-year-old ring-bearer? There are still many other elements to consider, however, before inviting young children to participate in your wedding. The first thing to examine is exactly what your motivation is for wanting children in your ceremony.

If you are going for the ooh's and aah's, you may want to reconsider the idea. Remember that young children do have minds of their own. When they find themselves with an audience of 200, they are likely to do any number of things, none of which may be what you had in mind.

Quite often, children get nervous. Some stand sullenly at top of the aisle while all of the bridesmaids whisper "Go" and the audience giggles. Others get halfway down the runner, spy grandpa, and go running into the aisles. A few make it all the way to the front before they get teary-eyed and scream for mommy.

Children can be a wonderful addition to your ritual. If you wish to include them in your union because they are an important part of your lives together, then by all means, do so. Just keep in mind the following considerations.

The overall tone of your wedding. If you are shooting for an elegant event, you may want to limit the number of child participants to a single ring-bearer and a single flower girl. The more children that are involved, the higher the risk of confusion.

Which children to involve. How do you diplomatically include your one sister's well-behaved three-year-old and not involve your other sister's five-year-old brat? One solution is to appoint them different duties. The five-year-old could, for example, act as an usher with the sole duty of seating Grandma and Grandpa. Another possibility may be to only include children of a certain age group or close geographical location so that they may have more time to rehearse their roles. If some of your family's children are invited to participate and not others, ask their parents to explain the reasons to the kids prior to the event, so that the excluded children understand that they are no less valued members of the family.

The children's families. Before asking children to participate, are their families able to absorb the cost of the costumes, as well as the rehearsal time involved? Junior's involvement in your wedding is really his parents' responsibility. Be sure that his family can honor your request prior to getting the child excited about the possibility.

Children may be a precious part of your wedding ceremony and memories. Just be sure that you are including them for the right reasons, and that you are not expecting too much from the tiny tots' attention spans.

75.

Let Go of
"Non-Guest" Guilt

The elderly lady next door bakes you a chocolate crumb cake topped with the words "Best wishes" in icing. A former coworker buys you a set of monogrammed champagne glasses. Your mechanic waives the fee for your oil change. "Consider it a wedding gift," he says.

The problem? None of these people are invited to your wedding. How do you handle the "non-guest" guilt?

First, recognize that most of these people do not expect to receive an invitation. They are simply friends with giving natures who identify with your happy occasion and want to wish you well.

If you still feel a twinge of guilt or regret, you may consider inviting them—verbally—to your ceremony. Simply state that, although the reception has been necessarily limited to family, they are welcomed to attend the exchange of vows to be held at such-and-such a place and such-and-such a time.

This is not an option, of course, if your rituals and reception are being held in the same location—in which case, you may need to decide if these potential invitees should be on your "alternate list" of guests—you may be able to fit them in after counting the RSVPs from your initial list. Or you may need to ask yourself if these people are really friends enough to warrant any guest spots.

Remember that your guest list should be comprised of relationships that have been valuable in your past and will continue to be important to your future. Certainly, not *everyone* that you know and come into contact with will fall into that category. And your well-wishers do realize that fact.

So accept their heart-felt greetings with appreciation. Know that they do understand your dilemma. In most cases, they do not expect an invitation. Afterward, carry a wedding photo or two to share with them. And let them know how much you enjoyed the cake, the champagne glasses—or the oil change.

76.

Consider Practical Ways
to Trim Expenses

Some brides-to-be may find that they need to make major revisions to their wedding plans in order to obey their budget. Others simply need to shave off a few dollars here and there. For those who need to shave, here are some suggestions.

Rather than hire a photographer or videographer to capture the entire day on film—from the primping at home to the last dance of the evening—consider booking him for just the ceremony through the start of the reception. You may be able to save nearly half of the photographer's daily fee.

Is it necessary to have all of your cousins as bridesmaids? Cutting your attendants' list in half may save you hundreds of dollars in flowers, gifts, and rehearsal dinner meals.

Reevaluating your floral needs may be one of the quickest ways to save money. Using flowers that are in season; keeping bouquets simple and elegant; using potted plants for centerpieces; and picking up fresh-cut flowers instead of ordering arrangements are all budget-shrinking options.

A quick look at your expenditures will probably reveal that the majority of the funds are dedicated to the reception. Among these, meals and beverages are often the most costly. Break down each of these numbers for ways to economize. Skipping the sorbet and limiting the bar to beer, wine, and soft drinks may add up to minor changes and major savings.

Keepsakes can be cute. And expensive. All that little paraphernalia, such as guest books, printed napkins, engraved matches, and so forth can add up quickly. Really think about what is necessary and what you will never miss when you cross things off of the "must have" list.

77.

Learn to Compromise

Your wedding day is *your* day. As such, it should be designed around your dreams for a lifetime of memories. It is imperative that you and your groom not deviate on anything that you feel strongly about. But you may want to ask yourself, "What exactly is it that we feel strongly about?"

Will it really matter ten years down the road that your mother and mother-in-law-to-be wore different-length dresses? Is it so terrible if the band plays a couple of golden oldies for your grandparents to enjoy? Must the cake be hazelnut-flavored if your maid of honor is allergic to nuts?

Many issues may seem to be earth-shattering decisions in the moment. But what impact will these particulars make on the overall impression of the celebration? Is it possible to combine what is important to a loved one with your own desires? In the end, you'll feel happier that you were able to have those that you love around you, and the chance to give something back to them, as well.

78.

Let Go of Pre-Wedding Conflict

At one time or another, you may find that organizing a wedding will take its toll on the relationship between you and your mate. Details and deadlines can be mind-boggling. There are things that will go wrong. Perhaps some plans don't work out as intended.

In-laws and relatives may have strong opinions regarding the way things should be handled. Quite often, these may conflict with your own ideas. Add in lack of sleep and anxiety about the life changes that you're about to make. It's enough to make the most good-natured person turn a little grumpy. Imagine what it can do to those of us who are not always as even-tempered as we would like to be. If you find yourself asking, "Why am I marrying this impossible man?" it's time to take a breath and step back.

First, recognize that you may be acting a bit jumpy yourself, lately. Have you been snapping at your mate? Or blaming him for his family's actions? Your own behavior is likely to be mirrored by your partner's attitude toward you.

Second, remember that as women, we tend to talk our way through our frustrations. We usually feel better afterward. But often, men try to *fix* problems—especially ours—as opposed to discussing them. If you are constantly frustrated about things that he cannot fix, he may become frustrated himself.

Also realize that the more time you spend planning your wedding, the less time you spend focused on each other. Your mate may feel neglected and need some reassurance.

With your own behavior in mind, it is important that you then listen carefully to what your partner has to say. Perhaps you have been arguing for no good reason. If you spent the night in a heated debate about whether or not to include the "Hokey Pokey" in your music lineup, you may both just be unloading some stress onto each other.

Every one of us needs to be heard. And most of us need to blow off some steam now and then. Recognize the difference between the two, and let go of pre-wedding conflict.

79.

Approve Even if
They Disapprove

All of our friends and family will be completely overjoyed at the mere announcement of our impending nuptials, right? Probably. But there may also be that stray someone who, for one reason or another, is not excited about your union. There may even be a couple of people. Or (and let's hope not) there may be an entire family that does not approve of your marriage.

Your parents may not believe that you are ready for such a commitment. His parents may dislike the fact that the two of you plan to move to another country after the celebration. A friend may not be convinced that your union will last. Adult children are hurt that you are even considering remarriage after the death of your spouse.

In most cases, this concern—though perhaps misguided—is born out of love for you, your betrothed, or both. Don't we all want those that we care about to be happy?

At times, it may be difficult to keep these protests in perspective. But rather than take these doubts personally, as attacks on you or your mate, understand them for what they are. Human beings are naturally suspicious of change. In time, their worries will wane.

Assure your objectors that you understand their concerns. However, you and your groom have obviously already made your own decision. Be firm in letting them know that you want them to share in your joy, but you will not tolerate negative comments or actions.

Then, unless the naysayers attempt to sabotage your plans in some way, try not to hold a grudge. Behave with your usual grace. Hold your head high, and let time prove them all wrong.

80.

Treat In-Laws
with Respect

Many brides have the opportunity to nurture a close relationship with their in-laws. They are the fortunate ones, with solid foundations to steady any conflicts that may arise during the planning process.

But some women traverse a fairly rocky relationship with their relatives-to-be. For them, organizing a wedding may be the perfect opportunity for a fresh start with the groom's family. Let the in-laws know that they are important to you; that you want them to be part of your upcoming life with their son, brother, or father. Let go of the past, and move ahead with future happiness.

No matter how well you do or do not know your new relatives, and regardless of how well you may like or dislike these people, remember that they do deserve a special degree of respect. After all, they may have raised—or at the very least, are related to—the man with whom you fell in love.

Even if you find their suggestions to be a bit off-the-wall or their methods a little pushy, maintain your calm. Remember that they are trying to figure out how you fit into their family equation in the same way that you are working out how to fit them into your new life with your groom.

Sometimes, just giving your future in-laws the opportunity to voice their opinions and desires is all that you need to forge a relationship. If they feel considered and taken seriously, they may be satisfied. Then you can feel good about yourself, and move on to making the decisions by yourself.

81.

Honor Your Mother and Father

It's an old joke. "Mother, when do *I* get to plan *my* wedding?" pleads the exasperated bride.

"Just as soon as your own daughter gets married, of course," replies the mother.

Planning a wedding can bring parents and children together, but they can also drive each other crazy during the process. Have patience with your parents, and respect their opinions as much as you respect them.

Chances are that your folks may be paying for—or helping you to pay for—the celebration. Additionally, you may be asking them for a whole lot of assistance with other aspects of the organizational process. They are probably already involved in your wedding preparations, and have all sorts of opinions on how things should be run. Even when their suggestions seem overbearing, maintain communication. You never know when one of their crazy ideas will turn out to be right on target.

82.

Don't Complain to Him
about His Mother

If we're lucky, our new mothers-in-law are helpful, charming, and welcoming people. But one doesn't need to look beyond a few advice columns to find that not all in-laws are saints. Those women who are driven to unburden themselves in print, however, are at least headed in the right direction. It is far better to discuss your female-to-female battles with your friends rather than your groom.

A man cannot stand the thought that the two most important women in his life—his mother and his bride—do not get along. Furthermore, no one likes to hear disparaging remarks about their mothers. This is true, no matter how many times we may complain about our own mothers. We simply do not want to hear someone else do it.

Yes, he needs to be (briefly) appraised of any major conflict which you may be having difficulty resolving. Do this gently, without blame or accusation. Just let him know the facts. You may tell him that you are uncertain of the solution. Do not be insulted if he doesn't respond.

If your husband-to-be is typical, he will choose to stay out of your disagreements completely. He may say that he doesn't want to hear about it. Or he might listen to and console the both of you—and then let you work it out for yourselves.

Your fiancé may offer to speak to his mother, but do not expect it. Conversely, he may even side with her. If he does, do not take it personally or turn the argument into some type of in-law vendetta. He may be feeling suffocated. Or he may honestly feel that you are the one being unreasonable. And perhaps you are.

Unless your beloved habitually supports his mother's decisions over yours (in which case, you will be facing greater problems down the road), do not expect him to choose sides. In fact, don't even put him into the unfair position of feeling as though he has to choose sides. Blow off steam to your girlfriends. Let them give you advice. They are your best resource, since they're already on your side. After all, it's not *their* mother that you're complaining about.

83.

Handle Exes Graciously

Today's families often consist of an extended mixture of blood relatives, their spouses and families, and even ex-spouses and their families. Just because a couple may have split up doesn't necessarily mean that their relationships with the rest of the family have ended. This is especially true when the couple has children together.

That child may actually be you. If your biological parents, or the parents that raised you, have since divorced, whom do you invite to gatherings? The answer, of course, is up to you. Do not feel that you must exclude one or the other if both people have, and continue to play, an important role in your life.

Whether or not to invite other family member's ex-spouses and partners depends on that loved one's situation. It is true that blood is thicker than water, and you may need to be especially sensitive to the needs of your immediate relatives.

Keep your family's feelings in mind, but also do not allow yourself to be blackmailed. Remember that anyone who threatens that they "will not attend if you invite so-and-so" is putting their own emotions before yours. Assure the attempted blackmailer that you want them to share in your day—however, it is their own choice if they do not attend.

You may be especially touchy if the ex in question is your groom's—or vice versa. First, ask yourself what your (or your groom's) motivation is for inviting this person to your wedding. Do you simply want to flaunt your newfound happiness in front of your ex-husband? Or have you honestly remained friends? Do you honestly want the best for each other?

Children, of course, add a whole new element to the equation. And if either one or both of you have children from a previous marriage, those other parents deserve special consideration. Although every situation is different, if the children are participating in the wedding procession, it is in good taste to invite the remaining parent. After all, you and your groom will most likely have some type of relationship with this person for years to come. Even when young children are merely guests, inviting the ex is not only gracious, it is practical, since they can help to take care of the kids at a time that you and your partner will want to focus your attentions on each other.

Ultimately, deciding whether or not to invite estranged relatives is highly personal. It is an issue to be discussed, and agreed upon, by both you and your spouse-to-be.

84.

Work with Your Coworkers

There seems to be only one thing on your mind these days. And your coworkers have noticed. Most of your office mates will be excited for you. They will probably understand if you take a few extra minutes at lunch to stop for a fitting. Many will look the other way if they catch you browsing through a bridal catalogue at your desk. And few will object when you call the caterer on office time.

However, be careful not to take advantage of their tolerance. When you start to skip the staff meetings, they'll talk. And if you shirk your responsibilities or drop the ball, your coworkers may even shout.

While it is not a good idea to volunteer for any additional assignments at the office right now, be sure that you are still pulling your professional weight. In today's society, where nearly everyone feels overworked and underpaid, slacking off gets noticed—quickly.

If, despite all of your best efforts to juggle work and wedding, you find that you are shortchanging one or the other, it is time to step back and prioritize. Have you asked your friends and loved ones to help organize your wedding? Many of them are waiting for your phone call. Is it possible to schedule fewer hours at the office and still handle your duties? Can a colleague pitch in and help out with your workload? Surely there are people to whom you have lent a hand in the past who would be willing to return the favor.

Perhaps you need to schedule a few days away from the office to nail down some wedding details. Many brides are tempted to reserve all of their vacation days for the honeymoon. Then they wish that they had more time to themselves for wedding preparations. A couple of free days during the week leading up to the ceremony, along with a few days (if not the full week) immediately preceding the wedding, could be a godsend.

If you have no paid leave time available, you may want to consider taking a couple of unpaid days off. Talk to your boss. Be honest. Let her know that there are some loose ends that need to be tied up before your wedding and you are afraid that that time will interfere with your work. Chances are that she has already noticed and will appreciate your candor. Your boss may even give you a couple of vacation days—or half-days—as a wedding gift.

However you choose to handle the preparations leading up to your celebration, be sure not to shortchange your job. Remember that you will be facing your coworkers again after the honeymoon is over. Why not make it a pleasant reunion?

85.

Be a Little Selfish with Your Time

Your relatives have just arrived in town, and they want to take you and your husband-to-be to dinner. Ditto for your old college roommate, your best friend, and your spouse-to-be's cousin.

On one hand, you probably do not get much of an opportunity to visit with your faraway friends, and you can't wait to play catch-up. Many of us will start to schedule social outings with these loved ones before they even make their travel reservations. If you find yourself doing this and filling in your already packed agenda, stop.

It's easy to over-commit three months before the event. You assume that all of the items on your wedding checklist will be neatly crossed off, and you will have plenty of time to socialize. Unfortunately, this is rarely the case.

There are certain details that can only be taken care of in the last week before the ceremony. You can also count on a few last-minute glitches. You will also need some extra rest leading up to your big day.

Although it would be wonderful to have a one-on-one evening with each one of your dear, visiting guests, this will most likely be an impossibility. It is more likely that you will find yourself in severe need of a few extra hours to prepare, and a little quiet time during your final planning stages.

Remember that you have already devoted an evening to many of these folks during your rehearsal and rehearsal dinner, as well as several hours on the day of the wedding itself. You may have also committed time to a bridal shower and a bachelorette night. That is three — four? five? — days claimed.

If you have strong feelings toward additional time with friends, try scheduling one family dinner or a single sorority luncheon to chat with those loved ones. Reserve the time and the restaurant well in advance so that you can advise people who call ahead of the arrangements.

Try being a little selfish with your time in the beginning. It may save you from breaking dates in the end.

86.

Bid Farewell to Your Old Lifestyle

Right about now, your nesting instinct will probably be in overdrive. There is a part of you that can't wait to put all of this wedding craziness behind you and snuggle into your new life with your honey.

Before you agree to "honor and cherish," take a few moments to reflect on the freedoms of your soon-to-end single life. In a few days, weeks, or months, the planning will all be over. You'll have had your day, and then will (hopefully) have the rest of your life to wallow in the joys of marriage.

Soon, you may start a family together, which requires an even deeper level of commitment and responsibility. Revel in these last few hours of independence. Do something just for you.

Sharing your life with someone that you love is a wonderful feeling. Still, in a few years, you'll no doubt look back on these days of freedom with a particular fondness. Make the most of them by enjoying those things that you do just by yourself.

87.

Embrace the Changes Ahead

Soon, you will be officially related to your favorite person. There will be someone by your side to share your dreams. You'll have a hand to hold when you are scared. And someone will be around to bring you soup when you're not feeling so well. Doesn't that sound wonderful?

Still, it is a virtual certainty that at some point, the wedding details will feel overwhelming. You may start to wonder why you ever wanted to get married in the first place, much less plan a stage show for 200 people. Whatever were you thinking?

That's simple. You were thinking that you had found your perfect mate. Although he himself is not perfect, and neither are you, you are good together. You may or may not have tired of the single scene. But you were plainly ready to commit to a deeper relationship.

You were thinking that of all the men you have met and perhaps dated, this is the one whom you chose to love. Yes, love. How long did you spend searching for the right person to love?

And you were thinking how nice it would be to have a live-in friend to listen to your little triumphs and struggles of each day; a continuous travel companion; a soul to discover—and grow with—through the years.

When the wedding preparations take on a life of their own and you start to wonder if it's all worth it, remember the true purpose of the festivities. This is a celebration of your love and the union of your lives together. And that, most certainly, is worth all of the chaos that it may bring.

88.

Defend the "Sacred Week" of the Ceremony

There are only seven days to go. Six...five...four... By this time, you will be feeling one of two emotions. (That is, of course, in addition to the millions of other emotions that you have been experiencing since the day you said "yes.") Either you can hardly believe that all of your hard work has finally come to an end—in which case, those minutes until your big day will be ticking by far too slowly. Or you are completely panicked by the thought that you only have a few days to get everything done. How will you ever do it all in time? Is it too late to postpone?

Obviously, you want to shoot for the first position. The second will only lead to fatigue and anxiety, which as we all know, can only be hidden with a very thick veil and does not photograph very well.

Recognize that your agenda during the week before your ceremony is already quite crowded. There are certain appointments and obligations that absolutely must be scheduled during this time.

These may include providing a final guest count to your vendors, keeping your beauty appointments, hosting a bridesmaids' luncheon, and attending the rehearsal and rehearsal dinner.

You will also have special projects for the week, such as wrapping the attendants' gifts, packing for your honeymoon, and surviving the day before the wedding.

Even if you have taken a vacation day or two from work, which is highly recommended, you will find that the minutes of each day right before your wedding ceremony are quickly claimed.

And then there is sleep—that precious commodity that you may have actually forgotten about during the previous few weeks. Suffice it to say that a few hours of shuteye will keep you from turning into a cranky, puffy-eyed person whom even a black veil and the best photographer could not make look good.

To avoid the sleepless syndrome, take care of every task ahead of time. Before the week of your wedding, be sure that all of your final fittings and final details have been confirmed. Deliver all deposits and preferences to your vendors. Confirm that all arrangements have been made for out-of-town guests.

In short, defend your time during the week before the ceremony at all costs. Those precious moments need to be yours to rest up and sparkle on the day of your wedding. Consider the week as sacred. Take care of business and personal obligations beforehand so that during the countdown hours, you may focus your energy on you, your rest, and your own peace of mind.

89.

Survive the
"Day of" Emergencies

Ask any successful event planner what her secret is and she may well tell you: "Each event has its emergencies. The trick is to prepare for them."

"How," you may ask, "does one *prepare* for an emergency?" Simple. Accept that they will occur. Then give yourself the time to deal with them.

There will probably be many snafus that come up throughout your wedding preparations. However, the ones that rear their ugly heads the day or two before your wedding rank as emergencies. Clear the day before your wedding to handle these occurrences. Then expect to head into battle.

The tuxedos haven't arrived from the tailor as scheduled? You may spend the day tracking down the wayward garments. Your maid of honor's flight was cancelled and she may not be able to make it on time? You will need to appoint an alternate maid of honor and a revised order of procession. The deejay is sick with the flu? He should have specified an alternate in his contract, but if not, you will be one busy woman the day before your wedding.

Not all emergencies are created equal. But they are created. Try not to leave any detail to the last minute. You will need that day for any other emergencies that come your way.

90.

Prepare a Bridal Emergency Kit

Along with the pearl necklace, rhinestone hair clips, and white, silky stockings comes another popular bridal accessory: the elegant purse—that teeny beaded bag with enough space to carry, perhaps, a short comb. Formal purses tend to be so small that some brides prefer to skip them altogether. After all, what items are so important that a person cannot possibly forgo them for the span of five to six hours?

Remember that during that time span, two hundred pairs of eyes and a camera lens will be focused on you. All the while, your makeup will become increasingly smudged from crying, hugging, and kissing. Your stomach may be doing cartwheels. And something is bound to run, tear, or rip.

But before grabbing that monstrous canvas bag from your closet, loading it with supplies, and then slinging it over the delicately beaded shoulder of your wedding gown, try delegating the task of preparing a "bridal emergency kit" to a friend or family member.

Ask this friend to collect a kit of the items that you or your bridesmaids may need during the ceremony and reception, and to keep track of its whereabouts. Don't be surprised if throughout the course of your celebration, this person becomes as sought-after as the bride herself.

The bridal emergency kit may contain, among other things: your cosmetics, if they are not carried elsewhere; extra stockings; antacid; adhesive bandages (a lot of them for blisters); hairspray; breath mints; toothpicks (or better yet, small toothbrushes and toothpaste); eye drops; safety pins; a small sewing kit; club soda for stains (this can be gathered from the bar, but it is a good idea to keep a bottle in the ladies' room); powder; spray deodorant; tissues; nail file; nail glue; comb and brush; and most importantly, aspirin for the headache you'll have when you've taken care of the last emergency!

91.

Avoid Panic
with Practice

It's the eve of your wedding. You're down to the final steps—the rehearsal, the rehearsal dinner, and then the event that you've planned for last few months. Heady, isn't it? If you're like most brides, you will be feeling downright giddy today—just like a young teenager at her first school dance.

Try to set aside the joking, however, just long enough to pay attention at the rehearsal, and be sure that your attendants focus on the instructions, as well. After all, there is actually a reason for the rehearsal. Even the simplest of ceremonies can greatly benefit from a once-through.

Your officiator will instruct you in the procedure. Remember that he has presided over many rehearsals. He understands the mood and atmosphere. Quite frankly, he expects about as much attention as a flight attendant gets when she demonstrates to passengers how to buckle a seat belt.

Make it a point to ensure that everyone—including special acts, such as readers and singers—knows their cue. Be especially vigilant with children that may be included in the ceremony. Not only should young kids practice their strut down the aisle, but they also need to know that they are expected to be on their best behavior for the remainder of the ceremony. In their minds, if they are allowed to have playtime during the practice run, why shouldn't they expect to do the same during the real thing? Twenty minutes of everyone's concentration now will save you endless moments of anxiety tomorrow when you're standing at the altar, hoping that everything proceeds as planned.

92.

Relax for the
Rehearsal Dinner

The rehearsal dinner is often a couple's last chance to take a deep breath and let their hair down before the "big day." It also reminds the soon-to-be newlyweds that their wedding truly is a family event.

This dinner, traditionally hosted by the groom's parents, may be treated as a picnic brunch or a black-tie affair. It is a time for newly merging family members to get together in a relaxed setting. Many of these relatives may be meeting for the first time. Others will see loved ones that they have not seen for years.

Typically, the rehearsal dinner guest list includes the wedding party and their spouses or dates, parents, grandparents, the officiator (and her spouse), the organist or soloist, and any other family members whom you wish to include. Written invitations are only necessary for formal affairs. Some families also include any out-of-town guests that they feel it is their obligation to entertain.

Rehearsal dinners tend to be very festive occasions. They are marked by toasts from the groom's father and the groom himself. They are often the time that the bride and groom present their attendants with gifts of appreciation.

Now is when you need to forget about the details. Release your anxieties and tensions. You've made all of the preparations that you can, and your only job at the rehearsal dinner (after you've made a round of introductions) is to relax.

If you and your spouse-to-be take this time to enjoy yourselves and the company of your loved ones, every one of your guests will relax in your presence and have a good time. And that is, essentially, the purpose of the rehearsal dinner.

93.

"It's in God's Hands Now"

You open your eyes on "your" day and take a deep breath. It's the moment that you've been dreaming about and planning for most of your life. By now, you've attended to every possible detail. There is no room to worry about what may or may not be done. There is nothing more you can do. The rest is in God's hands now.

Regardless of whether you attribute your success to the god of your faith or the "god of pre-planning," you can expect some sort of test. Recognize that the destiny of your march down the aisle is no longer in your control. All that you can control now is your frame of mind. That requires two things: rest and nourishment.

Try to get some sleep the night before your wedding. Appoint yourself a strict bedtime, take a glass of warm milk with you, and give it your best shot. In the morning, do not allow yourself to skip breakfast, no matter how loudly those butterflies in your stomach may protest. You will be thankful for the energy later in the day.

Once you have ensured your physical well-being, prepare yourself mentally. There may be a surprise or two waiting in the wings. Accept it as fate. Your hairdresser called in sick today? The new girl will probably give you a better "do." The limousine didn't arrive because it's stuck in traffic? Perhaps that frustrating half-hour delay to find new transportation avoided a tragic highway accident.

We never really know what the universe has planned for us. Sometimes, we get a good story to laugh about in the future. Other times, we look back and realize that those frustrating snafus were actually blessings in disguise.

What we *can* do is appoint someone to run interference for all the little complications, and then surrender our control to a higher power. After all, we never really control the destiny of any day in the first place.

94.

Revel in Pure Bliss

Any veteran bride can describe the feeling of bliss that overtakes her on her wedding day. Whether it is her first marriage or her fourth, both she and the groom will be surprised by an undeniable aura of love and completeness.

Despite any anxieties over the upcoming exchange of nuptials, the couple-to-be will feel a peace that seems to be deeply rooted in their very souls. This emotion is a beautiful gift that deserves respect and begs for indulgence. Make it a point to take—at the very least—a few minutes of quiet time to absorb the moment.

Let your heart lead you to your favorite place of reflection. Choose your method of spiritual connection. Then take a few moments to simply be still and get in touch with your inner self. Indulge yourself in the elation that you feel from within. Allow yourself to be completely absorbed by this ecstasy. Not only will you carry its essence with you throughout the day, but you will be able to call upon it—and bask in it—throughout your marriage.

95.

Conquer Stage Fright

Just through that door await fifty to five hundred of your family and closest friends. They will all turn to stare as you skip down the aisle to change your life forever. What could possibly go wrong? It's not likely that you will trip. Or forget your lines. Or start to cry. Or...

The truth is that you may do any one of those things. But remember that every ceremony does have its little glitches. And, yes, those fifty to five hundred people are well aware of it.

The only thing that they are going to notice at the moment is a radiant you. And each one of them will take their cues from you. If you simply giggle when the officiator needs to remind you to kneel, then your congregation will giggle with you. If you lean over and kiss your groom on the cheek when he flubs his vows, your audience will feel your love and compassion. When you can't resist an ear-to-ear grin at the announcement of "Ladies and gentlemen, may I present this husband and wife," everyone in attendance will also don a wide smile.

Remember that the people who have gathered to witness your nuptials are your loved ones. They did not make this trip to judge you in any way. They are here to share with you, and they will respond to the ceremony in the exact same way that you do.

96.

There Is No Such Thing
as a Flawless Wedding

Which do you prefer to hear first—the good news or the bad news? Okay, here is the good news.

There is no such thing as a flawless wedding. That is also the bad news.

There are endless stories of wedding cakes that cracked on the way to the reception; attendants' flowers that didn't arrive until halfway through the ceremony; and the wedding bands that weren't tied down to the ring-bearer's little satin pillow. Some of those rings have never been found.

The trick is to simply make the event *seem* perfect. Accept that not everything will go as planned. Then hand off your wedding organizer (with all of those important phone numbers) to a trusted someone or two who can run interference for you.

Those people will ensure that the cake gets fixed before it is cut. They will steal the floral decorations off of the pew for you and your maids to carry down the aisle (and then later swap them for the real thing during photos). And they'll lend you their own jewelry for the ritualistic exchange of rings while scouring the place for your own ring.

Those one or two people will become your professionals for the day. Anyone can book caterers and entertainers. The important job is emergency management: having people who can handle all of the glitches so that the guest of honor — in this case, you, the bride — can focus on one thing: being the guest of honor.

97.

Dance the Night Away

Being a bride can be quite an exhilarating experience—especially on the dance floor. From the moment that the band strikes its first chord, everyone—from the handsome best man to your beloved father—will be lining up to dance with you.

This is a wonderful opportunity to create cherished memories by remembering the special men in your life. For instance, when was the last time that you danced with your grandfather? Have you ever danced with your husband's grandfather?

Unfortunately, many brides are too intimidated by dance floor performance anxiety to make the most of the evening. Relax. Spinning around the room doesn't require any fancy footwork. It just takes a little forethought and preparation.

In the weeks leading up to your reception, ask your father (or your spouse's father or an older friend) to teach you one basic dance—the box step. This is the most popular maneuver of the older generation. Also review the movements for any folk dances that may be particular to your heritage if you plan to include that type of music. Practice these basic, choreographed steps until you can hold a conversation and not think about what your feet are doing.

Then keep in mind the most important tip to graceful formal dancing—let the man lead. This is actually the most difficult part for novice dancers who want to control their movements. But once you are able to let go and follow your partner's direction, dancing becomes a very simple—and enjoyable—process.

Remember that your male guests will embrace the chance to dance with the guest of honor. They won't notice if you're not Ginger Rogers—but they will be thrilled when the beautiful bride requests their presence on the dance floor.

98.

Make Your Escape

The night is nearly over. Everyone is laughing and dancing. You're elated. You are also absolutely... exhausted. Your lips hurt from smiling and your feet are aching. You've greeted, kissed, and complimented everyone in the room. All that you want to do now is crawl into your husband's arms for a few savory moments of silence. It's time to escape gracefully.

There are essentially two ways to exit your reception. You and your groom can be sent off with a booming cheer. Or you can quietly sneak away. It's all a matter of preference and timing.

If you have no pressing after-party plans, you may choose to stay until the end. After all, this is your day. Why not enjoy every last minute of it? You may also opt to exit just after the last dance, amidst a group "good-bye" — usually accompanied by a shower of birdseed or rose petals — and climb into a car adorned with shaving cream and balloons.

If your wedding ends with the start of your honeymoon, it's perfectly acceptable (and not a bad idea) for you and your groom to duck out of the celebration, change into street clothes, and return to the site for your final good-byes. This allows you to maintain your schedule while letting your guests continue on with the festivities. Just be sure to give yourselves adequate time to say farewell. Once you are spotted in your regular clothes, you are sure to draw the crowd's attention.

The final option is to simply slip away quietly. For a new couple, eager for some solo time as husband and wife, this may be the method of choice. Before leaving, however, make sure that you have already greeted each one of your guests and that your escape vehicle is not currently undergoing its "just married" transformation.

You may wish to request that the band plays a special song for you and your mate to enjoy a final dance of your own. Don't let the deejay know that you are leaving, but do tell the photographer to capture that last dance on film.

If you plan to steal away, whisper a brief farewell to your parents, your maid of honor, and your best man. Do not allow any of them to talk you into "just saying a quick good-bye" to anyone—not a single soul. Word of your departure will spread quickly, and you will spend the rest of your evening trying to escape your own party.

Instead, steal away into the night. And don't look back. Welcome to your new life together.

99.

Conquer Wedding-Night Jitters

Let's face it. By the time today's woman marries, she may no longer be the picture of innocence that her mother and grandmother once were. Yet most brides still blush at the thought of their first night together with their new husbands.

Fantasies of epic romance may ensue when you imagine your wedding night—but that's a pretty tall order at the end of a jam-packed day. If you're young and energetic enough to make these dreams happen, go for it.

However, you may find that the excitement of the day has taken its toll. And believe it or not, you might just want to cuddle. If you don't believe that, round up a few of your honest girlfriends. Ask them about their wedding nights. Many will tell you that they were so exhausted that they don't remember much of it. And others may admit that their "big night" was a bit of a dud.

Why? It is simply because oversized ambitions do not necessarily combine well with undersized energy levels. Moreover, creating passion is a futile task if you're nervous about it. A romantic mood requires a relaxed state of being.

So therein lies the question: How can a woman be relaxed enough to enjoy herself, but not so relaxed that she falls asleep after a hectic day? The answer is to forget the fantasies, take things slowly, and listen to your body.

This night is special simply because it is your first night together as man and wife. The two of you may decide to pursue romance. Or you may choose to quietly enjoy each other's company while recuperating for the day ahead. If you are both tired, you may be surprised to hear that he is relieved to save the passion for the morning, when you are rested and relaxed.

Remember that there are no expectations for your wedding night. The only pressure that you are under is the pressure that you put upon yourself. If you just want to fall asleep in his arms, go right ahead. Many couples have done so in the past. And you don't have to tell a soul.

100.

Embrace the Femininity
of Your New Role

Something strange happens on a honeymoon. You look at this same man that you have been getting to know and growing to love for months or years in a whole new light. Your boyfriend is now your *husband*. He has legally agreed to be your protector and your companion for life, no matter how bumpy the road may get. That's a pretty impressive promise.

But what does that mean for you? Many of us have spent the majority of our adult lives proving our independence. *I am woman,* we have roared to society. *I don't need anyone. I can do it all by myself.*

Now that woman is a *wife* — and it is suddenly okay to need someone. You no longer have to do it all by yourself. Which means that soon, someone will see your vulnerabilities. Someone will be beside you when you awaken in the middle of the night and your roaring has softened to a purr. *I am woman.* And *I'm not always so sure.*

The point to remember is that someone will be there for you. Your man has just promised to do so. He has agreed to help you shoulder your world when it becomes too heavy. (Not only did he do this legally, he said it in front of his friends and your mother, so you know that he's serious.)

Sometimes, the most important part of honoring your own commitments to your loved ones is to accept their commitments to you. Embrace your own role as nurturer and companion to him while taking comfort in his new role as protector and companion to you.

It takes courage to surrender your doubts and fears to faith in your relationship, but doing so will allow you and your husband to move into a deeper, more trusting love. This is exactly what you have promised to each other: an everlasting companionship.